A Long Journey

THE HISTORY OF DERBY WEST INDIAN COMMUNITY ASSOCIATION (DWICA)

HANSIB

The Derby West Indian Community Association (DWICA)
acknowledges the support of the following:

First published in Great Britain by Hansib Publications in 2024

Hansib Publications Limited
76 High Street, Hertford, SG14 3TA, United Kingdom

info@hansibpublications.com
www.hansibpublications.com

ISBN 978-1-7395636-9-1

A CIP catalogue record for this book
is available from the British Library

Production by Hansib Publications
Printed in Great Britain

www.hansibpublications.com

CONTENTS

ACKNOWLEDGEMENTS

We wish to recognise and acknowledge some of the people who have served and contributed to the growth and development of Derby West Indian Community Association (DWICA), over the years.

- **Mr J. Gordon** – one of the first Treasurer of DWICA
- **Mrs Myra Williamson** – Committee of Management and Carnival stalls fundraising.
- **Mrs Cynthia Chin** – Committee Member, Cook and running Carnival Stalls as fundraising venture.
- **Mrs Carmen Lee** – Activities Supporter and providing Cake Stalls to support Carnival fundraising.
- **Mr Cleveland Chin** – Committee Member, Disaster Appeal Activist e.g., Hurricane Gilbert – securing equipment resources for hospitals in Jamaica. One of the Carnival Organisers, providing Ice Cream Stalls. One of our Founder Members of DWICA Credit Union.
- **Mr Gilbert Williamson** – Committee Member, Carnival Volunteer responsible for the Bar.
- **Mrs Hilda Douce** – Founder of DWICA Domino Club, responsible for its development as a competitive Board Game Sport.
- **Mr Lloyd George Hudson** – Committee Member, DWICA Tote Organiser and later responsible for DWICA Domino Club and the Carnival Bar.
- **Mr Sam Lee** – Businessman and entrepreneur - one of the most able Treasurer of DWICA. With George Mighty he produced the first comprehensive Constitution of the Association. He was the brainchild and one of the founder members of DWICA Credit Union and led the way to the 'buy-a-brick' initiative for the establishment of our Centre.
- **Mr Vincent Sewell** – member and activist who volunteered to run our bar (Social Club) very successfully at the early stages.
- **Mr Jerry Smith** – Member and Volunteer, representing DWICA in Derbyshire Schools. Instrumental in the establishment of Radio Derby 'Black Roots' programme.
- **Councillor Harrold Cox** – served on the Committee representing Derbyshire County Council and must be credited for the introduction of our Indoor Mat Bowling.
- **Willitz Gabbidon (d)** – DWICA Active Volunteer / Member; Secretary and Board Member of the DWICA credit union.
- **Milton Crosdale** – DWICA Active Volunteer / Management Committee Member. Instrumental in the development of DWICA building facilities (Phases 1 & 2). Active project team member of DWICA community projects.
- **Councillor Mrs Una Turnbull** – represented Derbyshire County Council on DWICA Management Committee and along with Councillor Harold Cox – supported and guide us regarding council matters.
- **Mr Lyndon Williamson** – a long serving member of the Management Committee and

a committed supporter of the development of our growth and activities.

- **Mr Jeff Blake** – a member who did a lot of leg work in trying to sell 'Buy-a-Brick' to members for the idea of establishing our own Community Centre.
- **Mr Roy (Gerald) Fraser** – Served on the Management Committee, ad hoc committees, and fundraising committees. A complete community person and one who supported DWICA activities/functions with the view of enhancing its growth and development.
- **Mrs Enid Francis** – Volunteer and Committee Member who was responsible for organising our Carnival Queen Show in the earlier years. She was also the first, Black Special Constable in Derby.
- **Mr Hirvin Barnaby** – long serving Management Committee Member, Carnival Marshall, and supporter of DWICA activities and functions.
- **Mrs Mavis Barnaby** – Committee Member. Our first Carnival Mama and the originator of our first Cultural Dance Group. Supported and contributed to DWICA in all areas of its activities.
- **Mr Robert (Bob) Murray** – Committee Member and responsible for continuing the development of our Saturday /Supplementary School. One of the Founder Member of and Chairman of the DWICA Credit Union.
- Members of our revered "Cultural Dance Group" – **Mrs Mavis Barnaby, Beverley Williamson, Joanie Hanson, Mrs Pearl Gordon** and **Minah Campbell**.
- **Pamela Layfette (Gabbidon)** – Committee Member – one of the Founder Member of the Credit Union and its Assistant Treasurer.
- **Mrs Yvette (Schloss) Gregg** – Member of DWICA Supplementary /Saturday School, Assistant Secretary and later Secretary of the Credit Union.
- **Mr Percival Gordon** – former Committee member

- **Mrs May Gordon (Bryant)** – DWICA Member and Volunteer, Cook for Carnival Troupe members and volunteers.
- **Mr Caleb C McBean** – served as Treasurer, Secretary and Vice-Chair
- **Mrs Aldressa Brown** – Committee member and Chair of the Sickle Cell support group
- **Mrs Olga Marr** – Committee Member, Sickle Cell Group Member, Represent DWICA and the Police Community Training Advisory Group.
- **Mr John Mullings** – Former Committee Member
- **Mr Rupert Clarke** – former Committee member
- **Mr Alney J Riddock** – former Committee member
- **Mr Vin Goulbourne** – former Committee member, bar manager and general repairs and maintenance to the community building.
- **Mrs Janet Goulbourne** – Committee Member and Bar Assistant
- **Mr George Davidson** – Former Committee member
- **Ms Virinder (Bimmy) Rai** – Conducted research/survey into the Health Needs of African and Caribbean Community in Derby for DWICA. This resulted in the establishment of DWICA's 'Active Health Lives Matter' project attracting funding from Derby City Public Health and Lottery Health Trust of some £190k over six years. She also helped DWICA secure additional resources for the organisation.
- **Mrs Sharon Sewell**, our volunteer fundraiser, who has raised thousands of pounds for staff and activities for DWICA over the years.

George Mighty
President & Chairman
Derby West Indian Community
Association (DWICA)

PREFACE

George Mighty, President & Chairman, DWICA

The initial inspiration for the publication of this book originated from the 'Across the Decades' exhibition organised by the Derby West Indian Community Association (DWICA) in 2016. The exhibition was to celebrate 60th anniversary of the formation of the association.

At the Exhibition, I met with Mr Arif Ali of Hansib Publications and during our conversation Mr Ali suggested that the material presented in the exhibition was worthy of being captured in a book. We discussed the proposal, and the process involved, but DWICA was unable to secure the funding required for the book project until now.

In 2019, an application for Windrush Funding for the book was unsuccessful. But thanks to Ms Charis Beoku-Betts, our 'Stronger Together' Project Manager who, in partnership with Laura Phillips, Head of Interpretation and Display at Derby Museums, made a successful application to the National Lottery Heritage Fund, for funding to stage an exhibition entitled 'The Centre that Powers the Road'. The application included funding for the book project which would enable us to catalogue and chronicle the work, progress and achievements of DWICA.

Whilst the Heritage and Legacy Project had Carnival as central to our achievements, the exhibition and the book have enabled us to demonstrate the arrival, settlement and achievements of the community of Caribbean people in Derby.

Through the activities they provide and services they offer, the Association and the Centre continue to be a "catalyst and rock" of the Caribbean communities that have settled in Derby.

George Mighty
President & Chairman
Derby West Indian Community Association (DWICA)

FOREWORD

Dame Margaret Beckett DBE

It's a pleasure and an honour to have been asked to write a foreword to this book commemorating and celebrating the Heritage and Legacy Exhibition staged by the Derby West Indian Community Association, (DWICA), in 2022 in partnership with Derby Museum whose support and professionalism made such a worthwhile contribution to the staging of the Exhibition.

It is particularly fitting that partnership was the process that led to the establishment of this enjoyable and impressive Exhibition since it is partnership itself that I find is my overriding impression both of the Association and of its contribution to the city and community of Derby.

One of my earliest memories, which has stuck in my mind, of events I attended as a new MP in the city some 40 years ago, was of a reception laid on by the Association – as I recall it may have been to celebrate Jamaican Independence Day.

Several things struck me forcibly – how vibrant and lively it was; that it was well attended and by people from all walks of life and all parts of the city and county; and that an attendee from the Jamaican High Commission in London told me of their belief, in the High Commission, that Derby was a place with good race relations and strong community cohesion.

Over the years I have witnessed many examples of community support and cohesion from the Association and its members.

All this is a consequence of the contribution, then and since, of the Windrush generation and those who have followed them.

I'm sure it is why, across the city, there was such a strong reaction to the recent scandalous mistreatment of members of that generation.

The Exhibition was both a reminder of our shared history and a celebration of the achievements of today's generation.

The book will be a lasting record and memento of the Exhibition itself.

Margaret Beckett

Dame Margaret Beckett DBE has served as the Member of Parliament for Derby South since 1983 and became Britain's first female Foreign Secretary in 2006

MESSAGE

Lance Dunkley

I am very, happy to learn that the DWICA have decided to write a book about its culture, heritage and history. It is our culture in every letter of the word and should be written by us for the legacy of future generations.

DWICA history of community development in Derby includes its flagship project that promotes community cohesion (something in which all ethnic groups could participate in) via "Derby Caribbean Carnival" whilst representing the cultural lifeblood of African Caribbean people.

Black people in Britain have always been an isolated group racially, culturally spiritually and otherwise. In their isolation they have remembered that during slavery they had to do something to keep them alive and that something was their African style carnival known as Shago, Kumina, and many other names.

Records reflect that Black people have been in Britain since Roman times and white racism followed them all the way which is evidenced in the transatlantic slave trade to which England government / aristocracy played it's part.

"The Draft proclamation on the expulsion of 'Negroes and Blackamoors', 1601" is an important document revealing that there must have been a significant proportion of people of different ethnic backgrounds living in Elizabethan England. But the proclamation asks for the deportation of black people, described as 'Negroes and blackamoors', from the realm of England. This was justified on the grounds that these people were viewed as Muslim 'infidels' who were draining resources needed by the Queen's 'own natural subjects' at a time of 'dearth' or hardship.

In the late 16th century, repeatedly failing harvests had caused an increase in poverty, starvation and vagrancy. In terms that might sound unnervingly familiar to a modern reader, the expulsion of black people was presented as a solution. In fact they were so small in number that their absence would have had done little to relieve English suffering". Source: British Library

In 1968 saw the Notting Hill first carnival and in 1975 Derby through DWICA embarked on a long-term project which was to put Derby on the map of annual Caribbean celebrations in England by developing a small Caribbean community festival into Derby Caribbean Carnival attracting international performing artists and having thousands of patrons attend.

This has proven to be critical in breaking down barriers and stereo-type profiling of the African Caribbean community in Derby.

The benefits of DWICA's work over the years are all important for all in the city as it has helped shaped community development in Derby.

That book in my opinion will be something to do with what is known as the "Restoration of Cultural Authenticity". I await its publication.

Lance Dunkley

THE RESEARCH TEAM

The Derby West Indian Community Association's research team took up the challenge to review and collate the organisation's historical documents and artifacts with the intention that they would be included in the 2022 exhibition at Derby Museum entitled 'The Centre that Powers the Road'. The information would also be included on the organisation's website and throughout the pages of this book. These records are to be held at the Derbyshire Records Office where they will serve as a reminder of the contribution made by members of the African Caribbean community (the Windrush Generation) that relocated from the Caribbean in the late 1940s and made their homes in Derby.

By embracing digital technology, DWICA has created an everlasting source of information that reflects the organisation's growth and development. It will be a valuable resource for students and academics, and those who are interested in the achievements and contributions made by Derby's Caribbean heritage community.

DWICA has held many cultural exhibitions in the past, these included, Caribbean Focus in 1986, which was a celebration of the Caribbean nations that are members of the British Commonwealth; Across the Decades, in 2016, in which the organisation celebrated 60 years of providing a community service; and 40 years of delivering Derby Caribbean Carnival in 2018.

In 2022, DWICA marked a milestone fortieth anniversary of the establishment of its community and cultural centre in Carrington Street.

It is important that the members of the community are also the authors of its own history, and in doing so, provide an authentic reflection of the journey made across the decades.

Berimma Sankofa
On behalf of the research team

Introduction

In 1955, members of the close-knit Caribbean heritage community decided to form an organisation devoted to the interests of the community. The intention was to deal with social and welfare matters and to provide a liaison with local agencies such as social services, the local council and the police. The foundation of the Derby West Indian Association (DWIA) aimed to address many issues, including:

- Matters affecting young women and their children
- Caribbean workers experiencing discrimination/abuse in employment
- Social welfare problems, such as housing
- Racial attacks and abuse towards members of the Caribbean community
- Police conduct towards Caribbean people
- General employment issues
- Addressing issues arising from poor service within the welfare state
- Out of school activities
- Assistance/advice in buying homes
- Assistance with communication with family and friends in the Caribbean

The Derby West Indian Community Association (DWICA) has been serving the local area ever since and also works to promote and celebrate the culture and heritage of Caribbean people in the city of Derby.

DWICA provides a range of services to the local community, including information and advice, support and training, cultural events and activities, and also works to raise awareness of issues relevant to members of the Caribbean heritage community. It works closely with the local authorities, local charities and other organisations to ensure that local needs are met.

The association is an important part of the local community and provides a safe and welcoming environment to celebrate Caribbean culture and heritage. It organises a range of events throughout the year, such as carnivals and festivals, which bring together people from all walks of life to celebrate the diversity of the local area. DWICA also works to promote education and training opportunities for young people from the local area, as well as providing mentoring and support for those who may need it.

A key aspect of the association is dedicated to celebrating and promoting Caribbean culture and heritage in the city of Derby, and it works to ensure that the voices of Caribbean people are heard and respected in the local area. It is also committed to tackling issues such as racism and discrimination, and works to ensure that all members of the local community are treated fairly and equally.

Over many decades, the Derby West Indian Community Association has become an important part of the local community in Derby and it is committed to promoting and celebrating Caribbean culture and heritage in the area.

Aftermath of the Second World War

Following the Second World War, the British government encouraged the immigration of Caribbean workers to Britain in order to help rebuild the economy and address the many labour shortages in the aftermath of the war. A variety of methods were used to attract a labour force from within the English-speaking Caribbean which included radio broadcasts, newspaper advertisements and word of mouth.

The first significant wave of Caribbean migrants began to arrive in the late 1940s. They were recruited to work in a range of industries, including manufacturing, transport, construction and the fledgling National Health Service.

Initially, around five hundred people from Jamaica, Barbados and Trinidad and Tobago answered the call. Most remained in London, with smaller numbers making their homes in other major cities across the country. Over the next two decades, hundreds of thousands of people from across the English-speaking Caribbean would migrate to what was once referred to as the 'Mother Country'.

At first, Caribbean migrants were welcomed by British employers, but they were soon often subjected to racism and discrimination, and were treated as second-class citizens. This was particularly true in the 1950s and 1960s. Despite this, the Caribbean workforce made a valuable contribution to the British economy in the aftermath of the war.

The events that shaped the history of Britain's Caribbean population during the late 1940s to the early 21st century were varied and complex. From the post-war period onwards, members of this community experienced a range of political and economic challenges, whilst also continuing to face racism and discrimination.

The end of the Second World War marked the beginning of the migration of large numbers of people from the Caribbean to the UK at the invitation of the British government.

It is estimated that as many as 500,000 Caribbean nationals eventually migrated to the UK between the late 1940s and 1970. This period was marked by considerable social and

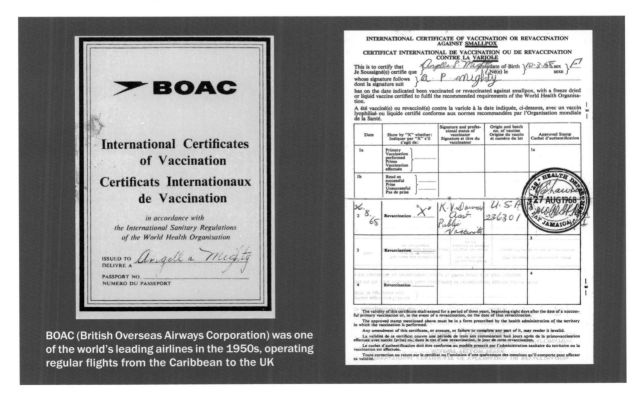

BOAC (British Overseas Airways Corporation) was one of the world's leading airlines in the 1950s, operating regular flights from the Caribbean to the UK

economic challenges as the new arrivals struggled to cope with British society.

The passing of the Race Relations Act in 1968, and the number of revisions of the Act since, aimed to put an end to certain forms of racial discrimination. However, in the 1970s, the rise of the Black Power movement was in direct response to racism and it incited political activism among Caribbean people living in the United Kingdom.

The 1980s saw the first Caribbean heritage MPs, Diane Abbott and Bernie Grant, elected to the House of Commons. And the 1990s saw the emergence of the concept of multiculturalism, which recognised the importance of different cultures in British society.

The end of the 20th century marked a period of significant changes in British society, with the emergence of a new, multicultural Britain. The Caribbean identity was no longer confined to one particular group, but increasingly celebrated amongst all Britons.

The events from the late 1940s to the first two decades of the 21st century have had a lasting legacy and resonance among Britain's Caribbean heritage population and the community has made invaluable contributions to every aspect of British society.

The Race Relations Act in the UK

The UK Race Relations Act was introduced in 1968, when the then Labour government, under Harold Wilson, sought to remedy the inequalities and injustices experienced by minorities in the UK. It provided civil and criminal sanctions against racial discrimination in the fields of employment, housing, education and the provision of goods and services.

Since its inception, the Act has been much amended and altered. The 1976 Race Relations Act brought more substantial changes, outlawing discrimination in more areas of public life, including the Civil Service, local government and other public bodies. It also created the Commission for Racial Equality (CRE) to monitor the Act's implementation.

The 2000 Race Relations (Amendment) Act extended the scope of the Race Relations Act to cover multiple discrimination, which is discrimination based on more than one protected characteristic at once, such as race and sex. A strength of this amendment is that it is capable of capturing struggles by minority groups, namely those from multiple backgrounds or identities.

The 2010 Equality Act – the latest amendment to the Race Relations Act – aimed to simplify and harmonise the previous race relations legislation into a single piece of legislation and further enhanced the Act's protection against multiple discrimination.

However, despite the many legal changes and advancements, racism in the UK still remains a reality. This is particularly pertinent when inequalities and injustices in areas not covered by the Act are considered, such as those related to policies and practices of police, prisons and the criminal justice system.

In addition, despite various legal changes, the UK remains unequal in some areas including housing and education, as illustrated in research from the Runnymede Trust in 2018, which claimed that there still existed 'ethnic disparities in educational attainment'.

Therefore, it is arguable that the Race Relations Act has not yet achieved its aims of creating a society in which all people are equal regardless of their backgrounds. This is something that needs to be continually addressed through the use of current and comprehensive anti-racism laws, and through the implementation of restructured approaches to the promotion of diversity and inclusion.

Ultimately, the Race Relations Act has made positive changes since its inception in 1968, but it needs to be continually addressed to fully break down the inequalities and discrimination that still exist in the UK.

PICTURED at a Derby Council House reception yesterday are the Mayor of Derby (Alderman Mrs. E. Wood) and Sir Laurence Lindo, High Commissioner for Jamaica, with the Town Clerk of Derby, Mr. N. S. Fisher (centre). The High Commissioner had a number of engagements in the Derby area yesterday.

Jamaican High Commissioner

West Indians did not come to live on State

TO suggest that immigrants from the West Indies came to Britain in large numbers in the 1950's to live on the benefits of the welfare state which they did not know in their own country, was nothing more than a wicked and malevolent lie, Sir Lawrence Lindo, High Commissioner for Jamaica said in Derby last night.

"Our contribution to the economic and social services of this country has surely been well established over the years," he said, at a reception and lecture held by Derbyshire Commonwealth Council at the Friary Hotel.

He said the majority of the 250,000 West Indians now living in Britain arrived at a time when there was plenty of work and a period of full employment.

They came seeking work and to better themselves—opportunities which they could not then find in their own country.

"They came to work, and that is what they have done. And it should be remembered that it has taken initiative and courage to transplant themselves 3,000-4,000 miles away to a strange country," he said.

SOCIAL FORCES

It was a misconception that West Indians wished to live among themselves in ghettos—these were the result of social forces not of their own choice.

He said all countries had to impose controls on immigrants, but what was asked of Britain was that immediate dependants of those already here should not be debarred from joining them.

The children of immigrants whose future lay in Britain where they were born must have a fair chance with equal opportunities of employment and housing and this was why the Race Relations Act was to be welcomed.

There were large areas of prejudice especially in employment and accommodation and though legislation was not the answer it went a long way to helping in a law-abiding country.

BLACK POWER

Questioned on black power, Sir Lawrence said: "The black power movement is not to be defended or excused, but it is something that can be explained and understood. But we regard black power as among only an infinitesimal minority."

Sir Lawrence was introduced by Mr. Maurice Chandler, East Midlands area chairman of the Conservative Commonwealth Council and thanked by Mr. Patrick Drury-Lowe.

PROBLEM OF WEST INDIANS IN BRITAIN

Mr. G. John, a member of the East Midland Conciliation Committee, spoke on the Race Relations Act to Derby West Indian Association.

He surveyed the pattern of West Indian immigration into the United Kingdom and some of the problems encountered by West Indians, especially in housing, employment and everyday life.

The president (Mr. Charles Hill) presided.

DERBY
Evening Telegraph CITY

Journey from the Caribbean to the UK

A typical journey of migration in the 1940s and 1950s began on board a cargo ship. These ships typically carried goods such as sugar and rum as well as passengers, and the journey could take up to three weeks, depending on the weather and the speed of the ship. Passengers were provided with basic amenities, such as food and sleeping quarters, but the conditions were often uncomfortable. However, the journey was considered to be relatively affordable.

For some, air travel was a quicker but more expensive option. One of the world's leading airlines in the 1950s was BOAC (British Overseas Airways Corporation), and it operated regular flights from the Caribbean to the UK. Flights departed from various Caribbean countries, including Jamaica, Trinidad and Tobago, Barbados and The Bahamas, and would then arrive at London Heathrow Airport. The duration of the flight was typically around 16 hours with multiple stops for refuelling.

Upon arrival in Britain, many faced a range of challenges, including language barriers, cultural differences, racial discrimination and the cold weather. Despite these difficulties, many people from the Caribbean managed to find work in a range of industries, including transport and the health service, as well as establishing their new lives in Britain.

Momentous arrival of the Empire Windrush

On 22nd June 1948, a ship carrying hundreds of passengers from the Caribbean arrived in Britain and changed the course of its history: the Empire Windrush. This voyage, and the people on board, marked an important milestone in the relationship between Britain and the Caribbean, and had far-reaching implications for the years to come.

The *HMT Empire Windrush*, a former transport vessel of the Royal Navy, had been requisitioned to make the journey from Jamaica

The NHS and the Caribbean contribution

The National Health Service in Britain is an iconic public service, rising as a beacon of hope against the pathos of war-torn austerity. Formed in 1948, it was the first system of its kind in the world, driven by a commitment to provide free healthcare to all regardless of means.

The realisation of the NHS owes much to the efforts of Caribbean migrants. As a part of the British war effort, the Caribbean had supported the Allied cause, and in response, the British government extended invites to these individuals to fill the severe labour shortages due to the destruction caused by the Second World War. These individuals were offered jobs in factories and public services, including the NHS. Caribbean migrants immediately began to make an essential contribution, particularly in the healthcare sector.

Today, the NHS is one of the most influential and enduring healthcare services in the world. It reflects the social values of the British people, combined with the commitment to care shared amongst Caribbean migrants and their descendants.

The NHS is still a source of comfort, understanding and dedication – qualities which truly describe the indomitable spirit of the Caribbean migrants and their enduring sacrifice.

It is important that their essential role in the establishment and success of Britain's beloved NHS is never forgotten. Their contributions are inextricably linked to the NHS and its legacy, and deserve acknowledgement and celebration to this day.

to the UK. On board were over 500 passengers from Jamaica, Trinidad, and other (now former) colonies, who had answered a call from the British government encouraging them to contribute to the country's post-war economy. Labour was sought in a variety of fields, from healthcare to engineering; and this group of passengers would become the first to be known as the 'Windrush Generation'.

These passengers were among the earliest large groups of people from the Caribbean to

Windrush Pioneer

Tom Hulce was one among the many Jamaicans that arrived in Britain aboard the *Empire Windrush*. He embarked upon the journey in response to an advertisement he had seen in *The Daily Gleaner* newspaper, such as one that announced: "Passenger Opportunity to United Kingdom" on board the Troopship 'Empire Windrush'. It stated that the ship would sail on 23 May and the fares were "£48 for Cabin Class" or "£28 on the Troopdeck". He is pictured on his wedding day.

enter the country in search of new opportunities and a better life. However, their arrival was met with a mixture of celebration and hostility.

The post-war period saw a number of discriminatory policies put into place, targeted at immigrants, especially people of colour. The 'No Coloureds' policy, in particular, made it difficult for Black people to find employment and decent accommodation – a struggle which endured for many years.

Despite the bigotry and discrimination faced by the Windrush Generation, their presence, and the arrival of those that followed, had a transformative effect on the landscape of Britain. Their invaluable contributions to the nation's economy, as well as to its cultural life, is unquestionable.

Today, June 22nd is marked in Britain as Windrush Day and it is held with great significance and symbolic importance by Caribbean heritage communities across the county.

Arrival in Derby

The Caribbean heritage community in Derby dates back to the 1950s and was largely based in the Normanton area. They brought with them a rich cultural heritage that has become a unique and vibrant presence over the decades.

Members of the burgeoning community would help each other and offer support wherever they could in the interests of community cohesion. They also had to adapt to their new lives in Britain and face all the challenges this would entail.

Time at weekends provided the perfect opportunity to engage with family and friends, both in Derby and across the country. They would share their experiences – whether good or bad – of issues related to housing, employment and social services, to name just

Bob Murray pictured in RAF uniform, left, in his early days. He was featured in the *Derby Evening Telegraph*, above and opposite, on 19th october 1995.

a few. It was also an opportunity to provide direct help to each other such as form-filling and letter-writing. Maintaining links with family and friends in the Caribbean was also essential and in most instances this was through writing letters to loved ones 'back home'.

Today, the Caribbean heritage community is well established in Derby. There are a number of Caribbean-run businesses, including restaurants, shops and other services along with a number of cultural organisations, chief among them being the Derby West Indian Community Association.

The significant contribution to the cultural life of Derby cannot be underestimated, with many local artists, musicians and dancers having Caribbean roots. In addition, a number of events and festivals have been established, such as the Derby Caribbean Carnival and the Derby Caribbean Food Festival, which celebrate the rich cultural heritage of the Caribbean.

Overall, the Caribbean heritage community in Derby has grown and flourished over the years and now makes a valuable and valued contribution to the city's cultural and economic life.

DERBY EVENING TELEGRAPH, Thursday, October 19, 1995 **13**

COUNTRY THROUGH WAR

heroes

OF all the outposts of the British Empire who answered the call to arms in the Second World War, it's the people of the West Indies whose contribution is perhaps the least recognised.

As Derby's West Indian community prepares to honour its ex-servicemen with a special exhibition, *MARTIN WELLS* talks to four black RAF veterans about their own experiences.

VINCENT Jones never intended to join up. A 19-year-old Jamaican, he only went along to the recruitment centre in September, 1944, to keep his pals company.

"I ended up taking the tests myself and, of course, I passed," he said.

He landed in Glasgow in the October. "It was cold but I had no regrets. I was proud to be in the RAF."

After square-bashing in Filey he was posted to munitions bases all over the country. "It was my job to arm the bombs before they went out to the squadrons," he said.

VINCENT JONES

While working at a maintenance unit in Alvaston, he met his first wife, a young Derby woman who lived in Abbey Street.

"After the war I went to college in Monmouthshire on a secretarial course," he said. "I gained my qualifications but, though jobs were plentiful after the war I couldn't get one, like most coloured people."

He settled in Derby in 1947 when he married his forces sweetheart.

"I'd never come across prejudice when I was in the forces, only when I was on leave and when I was demobbed.

"I can remember walking up the street and children looking at me in amazement and running off to tell their parents what they'd seen."

BOB MURRAY

FOR Bob Murray, born and raised in Guyana, answering the call to arms was the most natural thing in the world.

"As children we thought England was the land of milk and honey where the streets were paved with gold. We used to sing Land of Hope and Glory and Children of the Empire and really believe it ... we were more patriotic than the British," he said.

In late 1943, he responded to an RAF recruitment drive and by early 1944 he had landed at Glasgow aboard the HMS Carthage.

"When we disembarked it was foggy and cold but the welcome we received was very warm, especially from the WVS women who served us coffee, biscuits and sandwiches.

"It was the first time we'd been treated like this. Before, we were the black colonials, the servants."

An educated man, he began his RAF life in the accounts department of a training base in Wiltshire but soon became a vocational training instructor and rose to the rank of sergeant.

"A lot of the English people in the RAF hadn't had a basic education so I tutored people in the equivalent of the GCE," he said.

In the forces, he was largely protected from the discrimination commonly faced by black people after the war.

"In the forces you were protected by rules and regulations but when you came out you faced the cold blast of reality and it wasn't unusual to see signs like 'No dogs or niggers' in restaurants. Hotels would turn you away and even after attending church services, the vicar would say that they'd rather you didn't come back."

After the war, he trained as an accountant but found it impossible to get a job. "I got so desperate that I had my bags packed and was ready to go home, only to get a job with the Post Office Savings Bank the next day."

In 1960 he moved to Chesterfield when his department relocated and in the seventies he spent three years studying to be a teacher before moving to Derby and taking up a post at Littleover School.

Now 72, his bitterness has receded and, as chairman of the Nottingham branch of the West Indian Ex-Servicemen's Association, he has written a book about his experiences. "Two things blighted me in the days after the war — no job and nowhere to live. But I persevered ... I was put on this earth to make progress."

The reaction of Derby employers was hardly any more enlightened. "I went for jobs at the Post Office, at Trent buses, the banks and the railway but no one would take me on."

Eventually, he was taken on at Parker Foundry. "When I went there the foreman went around the rest of the workers to see if they minded working with me – none of them did.

"Even when I was taken on I was forced to work twice as long as everyone else before I was allowed to go on piece rate."

Vincent's first wife died in 1970 and he remarried three years later. Now 69, he lives in Milton Street and is recovering from a triple heart by-pass operation.

He retired from Parker Foundry eight years ago after 40 years working as a grinder and fettler.

Mr and Mrs Allen pictured, centre, on their wedding day in the 1950s. Like so many people from the Caribbean, they answered the call from the so-called 'Mother Land' in the years following the Second World War.

Pictured on their wedding day, Mr and Mrs Williamson arrived in Derby in 1962.

Mr Douce

The Percy's family wedding of one of the sisters

INDUSTRIA·VIRTUS·ET·FORTITUDO

Windrush Declaration

Derby City Council acknowledges the positive contribution made by the Windrush immigrants, many of whom were ex-service personnel, in the making of modern Britain.

The Council values the City's Caribbean community and its contribution which has made the City richer in heritage and new traditions.

The Council is committed to celebrating the cultural diversity of its citizens. We intend to demonstrate this by taking a lead in organising activities to commemorate the arrival in Britain of Windrush immigrants, some of whom became Derby's new citizens.

Mayor of the City of Derby

Leader of the Council

Chief Executive

Normanton Road, Derby, in the circa 1950s

Normanton Road, circa 1970s

CELEBRATION OF JAMAICAN INDEPENDENCE

Telegraph
10 August 1970

MEMBERS of Derby West Indian Association who attended a special event at Tiffany's, Derby, to mark the anniversary of Jamaican independence, received a message from the Prime Minister of Jamaica, Mr. Hugh Shearer.

Guests included the Mayor and Mayoress of Derby (Alderman Miss M. E. Grimwood-Taylor and Miss Elizabeth Garnett), and Mr. G. L. Coke, recruitment officer at the Jamaican High Commission, London, who passed on the good wishes of the High Commissioner, Sir Laurence Lindo.

Among the attractions was Derby's own West Indian pop group, "The Coolers."

First prize in the best dressed woman competition was won by Miss Hyacinth Wright, Miss Ann Williamson was second, and Miss B. Pouns third.

Derby visit by Jamaica High Commissioner

Derby EVENING-TELEGRA
22/12/69

MR. R. ASTON FOREMAN, Deputy High Commissioner for Jamaica, visited Derby to discuss with members of Derby West Indian Association Committee the problems of racial integration.

He also visited the Royal Crown Derby china works and the newly-opened Pear Tree Community Centre. He was accompanied by Mr. C. Hill, president of the association.

A few years ago Mr. Foreman visited Rolls-Royce Ltd.

DR WINT (centre) with the Mayor and Mayoress and Mr S. A. Walters, president of Derby West Indian Association.

Jamaican High Commissioner visits Derby

28-2-76

JAMAICA'S High Commissioner, Dr Arthur Wint, the Olympic track star turned ambassador, had a warm reception when he arrived in Derby yesterday to visit the town's West Indian community.

Dr Wint, who was the guest of the Derby West Indian Association, arrived in Derby from London, where he is permanently stationed, and his first call was at the Rolls-Royce Sinfin premises where he viewed development work and toured the factory.

Last night, at the Pennine Hotel, Dr Wint was welcome by about 150 West Indians, and also met invited guests. These included the Provost of Derby, the Very Rev R. A. Beddoes, Councillor Peter Regan, Colonel and Mrs Peter Hilton, the Rev Eric Smart and Mrs Smart, Mr Joe Cunningham, clerk to the justices, and chairman of Derby magistrates Miss E. M. Grasett. Dr Wint later left for a private party at the Havana Club.

INFIRMARY

Today he was visiting the Carib International Club, Homelands School, and was seeing the Mayor of Derby, Councillor George Salt. Then, after flying visits to the Derbyshire Royal Infirmary and British Celanese at Spondon, he was returning home.

Dr Wint's athletics career was crowned in 1948 when he won an Olympic gold medal in Helsinki in the 400 metres event. His interest in aeronautics stems from his career in the Jamaican Air Force, where he rose to Flight-Lieutenant.

Commenting on the visit, Derby West Indian Association Secretary Mr C. C. McBean said: "Dr Wint had been known to our association by name and reputation for so long that we had to meet him. He seemed to enjoy his stay in Derby, particularly the trip to Rolls-Royce. He was very impressed with the RB211."

Evening Telegraph *DERBY* [CITY]

DERBY EVENING TELEGRAPH, Friday, August 7, 1970   19

CHATTING at Derby West Indian Association independence celebration dance at Tiffany's, Derby, last night are (from left) association secretary Mr. C. C. McBean, Mr. L. G. Coke, recruitment officer with the Jamaican High Commission office in London, and Mr. M. S. Douglas (association vice-president).

LEFT: Members of DWICA's Management Committee, the Mayor of Derby and his wife, Members of Parliament and guests at a Jamaica Independence Celebration Event.

Derby train station in the 1960s

Derby bus station at the Morledge in the 1960s

International festival's all-Derby cast

August 1976

INDIA, Ireland, Serbia, Scotland, the Ukraine, the West Indies — and of course merry England — will be countries represented at an international festival of music, dance and drama at Markeaton Park on Saturday week. Yet all the participants come from Derby area.

The festival is presented by Derby Council for Community Relations with the object of creating deeper understanding between various groups in the community.

Contrasting with dances by Derby branch of the Scottish Association and Burns Club and the Turley School of Irish Dancing will be traditional dances from the Hoverlia and Werchavyna Ukrainian dancers and musicians, Serbian folk dances from the Ravna Gora group of Derby Serbian Association and dances from the Gujerat area of India and the famous Bhangra dance from the Punjab, performed by the Jugna Group of the Hindu temple in Derby.

Representing Derby West Indian Association will be Melvyn Fox and his one-man steel band and folk singer Cordell Spence.

Other items are modern Indian dance mime by Miss Anjna Sharma and her sister, and Morris dancing and a mummers play presented by Wilsthorpe Comprehensive School, Long Eaton.

If wet, the festival will be held in the Great Hall of Derby College of Art and Technology, Kedleston Road.

Independence celebrations at extended centre

JAMAICA'S 21st Independence Day was celebrated in style on Saturday by Derby's West Indian Community in their newly-extended community centre.

About 500 attended the celebrations at the Carrington Street centre with attractions staged by young people in the community during the day and an Independence Day dance in the evening.

Among the guests were Jamaica's deputy high commissioner Mr D. Anderson, Derby MPs Mrs

Margaret Beckett and Mr Greg Knight and Deputy Mayor Councillor Ron Longdon.

It was the first major function to be held in the extended £179,000 centre.

Many aspects of the West Indian community were on display during the day with music, art and literature on show. Among performers were the Hardwick School Steel Band and the Ajah drum and dance group.

Derby West Indian Association president Mr Solomon Walters explained that the celebrations were intended to raise money for the centre and display the West Indian Culture.

The association hopes to start a day nursery and day centre for young people at the community centre.

"We are hoping in due course to realise our aims," he said.

Drinking a toast to The Jamaican Indepence Day are (left to right): Jackie Fox, Carol Smith, Carol Fox, and Joanie Hanson.

INTERNATIONAL RECEPTION

21/11/69 EVENING TELEGRAPH

REPRESENTATIVES of the many nationalities which form the Town Committee of the Derby branch of the International Friendship League were welcomed to the Council House, Derby, by the Mayor and Mayoress of Derby, Alderman and Mrs. Tom Taylor, as pictured above, at a civic reception which formed part of 'People-to-People Week' activities. The Mayor is the branch president.

Visitors, including members of the Overseas League, West Indian Association, Women's International League of Peace and Freedom, and the Overseas professionals' Association, were shown the Council Chamber and civic treasures, and had tea at the Council House.

The event was attended by Mr. J. H. Christmas, chairman of the Derby branch of the Community Relations Board, and members of the Derbyshire Royal Infirmary and City Hospital staffs.

Nurse K. Lehal, of the Infirmary, presented a bouquet to the Mayoress.

8 **DERBY** EVENING TELEGRAPH, Monday, February 7, 1972

GUESTS and members of Derby West Indian Association, pictured at their dinner held at the Clarendon Hotel. Principal guests included the Rev E. Smart; Mr G. H. Scott, officer for community relations; Mr St C. McKenzie, regional welfare officer, Birmingham branch, Jamaican High Commission; Mr C. C. McBean, secretary, Derby branch, and Mr C. S. Hill, the Derby branch chairman.

BELOW: A return visit for the Mayor of Derby (Councillor J. J. Carty) from a soldier he met when he visited the 94th/12th Royal Lancers in Germany recently. With the Mayor and Major Tom Hill, Army careers officer (left), is Corporal Barry Brown, of 33 Highfield Road, Ashbourne, who is on leave and will also spend a week at the Derby Army careers office before rejoining his unit in Germany.

DERBY Evening Telegraph CITY

Derby market place in the 1960s

Derby market place in the 1960s

Evening Telegraph. 18/6/68

MR. SHAH (left) and Mr. Douglas.

Two coloured welfare officers for Derby

TWO Commonwealth nationals—both well known to Derby's immigrant population and others interested in Derby's overseas organisations — have been appointed as Education Welfare Officers by Derby Education Committee's Social Services Sub-Committee.

The two new officers, who were appointed yesterday are Mr. Abdul Rehman Shah, of 95 Litchurch Street, Derby, and Mr. Melvyn Stanbury Douglas, of 17 West Avenue, Derby.

A Pakistani, Mr. Shah came to Derby four years ago after serving in the Pakistan Army as a major. He has since been working as a machine operator with British Celanese Ltd., at Spondon.

During his 27 years' Army service—he was originally in the Indian Army—Kashmir-born Mr. Shah fought in Burma, was mentioned in dispatches and has been awarded four medals.

He is married and has three children, two sons and a daughter. His wife Rqueeda is a graduate of the Punjab University and a former school-teacher. She has recently been working as a doctor's receptionist in Derby.

ON RENT PANEL

Mr. Douglas is well known as secretary of Derby West Indian Association. He is a member of the East Midland Rent Assessment Panel, and an executive member of Derby Council for Community Relations.

has been a need for this type of appointment in the borough particular in the Pear Tree area."

'NO COLOUR PROBLEM'

But both aldermen emphasised that there had been no colour problem in Derby—"please do not mention that word," said Alderman Mrs. Mack.

The two recruits will work in a team of four welfare officers in a large area to the south of the town centre containing 26 schools with a school population approaching 11,000.

Mr. Shah said he was very pleased to be living in Derby, which was now his home. "All the countries in the world can learn something from the English people," he said.

Mr. Douglas, giving his reasons for taking the appointment, said: "I felt I should like to devote the rest of my life to helping other people as much as possible and I think I could make a contribution in this particular field."

He is married and his wife, Amy Joyce, is a ward sister at Pastures Hospital, Mickleover.

Jamaican-born Mr. Douglas came to Derby in 1957 and has been employed at British Railways Locomotive Works as a machinist, at Derbyshire Royal Infirmary as an operating theatre attendant, and at Derby Museum and Art Gallery.

Alderman Mrs. E. J. Mack, chairman of the Special Services Sub-Committee said: "We feel this is a good appointment and are looking forward to a happy relationship with these people."

Alderman Jeffery Tillett, chairman of the Education Committee commented: "There

JAMAICANS CELEBRATE INDEPENDENCE

17/8/73

Mr Phillip Whitehead, MP for Derby North, spoke on the good relations between Jamaicans and the English, at the Jamaica Independence Day celebrations at the Carib International Club, Derby, yesterday.

Mr Tom Douce, proprietor of the club, said things went very well.

"We were packed at about 8.30 and the music from Jimmy Mack and the Reason Why and the Cox International Sound was excellent."

Mr Douce made a speech on behalf of the Jamaican population, commenting also on the good relations over the years and the racial harmony enjoyed in Derby.

WEST INDIAN TRIBUTES TO DERBY MPs

TRIBUTES to the two MPs for Derby, Mr Phillip Whitehead and Mr Walter Johnson, for their help in the Rolls-Royce crisis, were paid by Mr Charles Hill, chairman of Derby West Indian Association, at the Jamaican independence celebrations at Tiffanys, Babington Lane, Derby, last night.

Mr Hill introduced the Mayor, Councillor Joe Carty, and the Mayoress, Mrs Carty.

The Mayor spoke about the part that Jamaicans played in the life of the community and mentioned that he spoke as a member of Derby Hospital Management Committee. He praised the many West Indian doctors and nurses who work in Derby.

SECOND TO NONE

Mr Walter Johnson said the record of race relations in Derby was second to none, a point confirmed by Mr Phillip Whitehead, who went on to congratulate Mr Hill and Mr C. C. McBean on their work for race relations in the town.

Mr Hill introduced Mr C. G. Coke, regional welfare officer, and representative from the Jamaican High Commission office in London.

Mr Coke spoke about the young and developing Jamaica and that they should make the most of all the opportunities offered in this country to help Jamaica.

Also present were Mrs Johnson; Mr and Mrs H. M. Shelley, Chief Superintendent of Derby County and Borough Police; Councillor and Mrs M. D. Thomas; and the Rev and Mrs Eric Smart, Vicar of St. Thomas's, Derby.

BEST DRESSED

A competition to find the best dressed lady was won by Miss Peggy Williamson, of 148 Cameron Road, Derby. Second prize went to Miss Shirley Johnson, of 31 Wilfred Street, Derby, and third to Miss Maria Wright, of 159 Portland Street, Derby.

PICTURED are young dancers swinging into the rhythm.

DERBY POLICE TO HOLD RACE RELATIONS COURSE

SENIOR police officers from eight forces are to attend a race relations course, organised by Derby County and Borough Police.

Leading authorities on community relations will lecture to the officers from November 29 to December 1 at The Hayes Conference Centre, Swannick.

Speakers will include Dr Marie Jahoda, professor of Social Psychology at Sussex University; Mr John Ennals, Director of the UK Immigrants Advisory Service, London; Dr Farrukh Hashmi, consultant psychiatrist at All Saints Hospital, Birmingham; Mr Dipak Nandy, Director of the Runnymede Trust; Mr G. H. Scott, Community Relations Officer for Derby and Mr Harry Ambler, Chief Constable of Bradford City Police.

Among topics to be covered are the work of the Community Relations Commission, racial discrimination and the law, the police and the immigrant, and future problems which may arise in absorbing a coloured community.

DERBY Evening Telegraph [CITY]

DERBY EVENING TELEGRAPH, Tuesday, November 25, 1969   7

CELEBRATIONS HAD AN ACCENT ON DIFFERENT NATIONALITIES

FURTHER events in the "People to People Week" were celebrated in Derby over the weekend, with a children's party at Normanton Junior School on Saturday afternoon, a West Indian night at The Garrick, in Friar Gate, a little later, and an all-faiths service on Sunday.

On all occasions, the accent was aimed at a good representation of different nationalities, and about 80 children went to the party during the afternoon, who were picked mostly from junior schools within the Normanton area.

The party was organised by the Derby branch of the International Friendship League and most of the children were about ten or 11 years old.

But while the International Friendship League were responsible for serving the teas, and received help from the Women's International League of Peace and Freedom, it was teachers from the local schools who helped entertain the children, under the organisation of Mr. J. Morris, Headmaster of Pear Tree Junior School.

The children played games and entertained each other with singing and dancing.

The West Indian night was also well supported with people of many nationalities, I am told, and with wine and cheese provided, the evening was quite informal.

All faiths

This event was organised by the Derby West Indian Association, and entertainment was provided by a few young West Indian men who played guitars while the visitors danced.

An all-faiths service, with readings from the Christian, Jewish, Hindu, Sikh, and Moslem scriptures, was held at the Presbyterian Church, Green Lane, Derby, to mark the end of the annual "People to People Week."

The service was conducted by the minister, the Rev. H. Mulholland, who also gave the address, and one of the elders, Mr. M. Castledine, who is a member of the International Friendship League (Derby branch) introduced a few of the items.

The service was designed to include all the faiths and about 80 people who attended had tea afterwards.

These events were the last to be held in Derby, where the "People to People Week" now an annual event, was celebrated during last week.

Derwent's Diary

GLYN KOPJAS (left) and his friend Donald Powell, are pictured giving a recital at the International Friendship League's children's party. Glyn has been studying the clarinet for 20 months and Donald for three months.

CORDEL SPENCE and Harold Smith are seen entertaining guests at the West Indian Association social at the Garrick Hotel.

DERBY EVENING TELEGRAPH, Thursday, August 6, 1970   15

COLOURED SCHOOL LEAVERS WILL WANT SHARE OF GOOD JOBS

FIRST - GENERATION immigrants came to Britain to seek work and almost any job was an improvement on their position at home. "But future generations will want a share of all the jobs—the better ones as well," says a report by Derby and Derbyshire Junior Chamber of Commons today.

"Accordingly equality of opportunity must be real and be demonstrated to be so to those about to commence their future careers," commence the report.

Statistical information in the report shows that in January, 1968, Derby's percentage of coloured immigrants in borough schools was 10 per cent. Excluding the London boroughs, this was only exceeded by Wolverhampton.

Even with the extension of the Derby borough boundaries, the January, 1969, figure was 8.1 per cent. And of the entire Derby population of 220,000 in January last year, five per cent. was coloured.

Well in excess

"The Derby proportion is well in excess of the national figure and demonstrates why the future of the Derby coloured school - leavers cannot be ignored," declares the report.

Entitled "The Integration of the Coloured School Leaver in Derby," the report is the work of the Chamber's Education and Youth Activities Commission.

The report expresses the firm belief that the answer to successful integration lies in equality of opportunity.

Offering various suggestions to employers, education departments and immigrants, the report comments: "By acting upon them we in Derby can demonstrate that our school leavers are expected to take up full citizenship with both equality of opportunity and responsibility, irrespective of colour."

No more problems?

The report comments: "With discrimination in employment made illegal by the 1968 Race Relations Act, the West Indian, Pakistani, and Indian school leavers in Derby should find no more problems than their other contemporaries in obtaining jobs and progressing in them. Or should they?"

To attempt to assess the situation, the Commission prepared questionnaires and talked to Derby employers and Trades Union Council representatives, borough education officers, the Community Relations Officer, the local Race Relations Board Conciliation Officer and the immigrants themselves.

Praise indeed!

During their survey, the Commission learned from an immigrant leader that: "Immigrants like the school atmosphere in Derby."

"Praise indeed for the Borough Education department. To achieve this with such a high proportion of coloured children in Derby schools can have been no accident," the report remarks.

Immigrant children who had no command of English were being helped to learn the language, and it was evident that there was "considerable personal dedication in helping the children far beyond the normal duties of a school teacher."

Each summer approximately 2,400 children left Derby schools looking for work, of whom about 100 at present were coloured. In future this number would increase and might reach 300.

"As to problems in placing coloured school leavers in employment a distinction rapidly became apparent between West Indians and Asians on both attitude and ability."

Not perfect English

Action was being taken in Derby to strengthen West Indian participation in Parent-Teacher Associations and similar organisations, to assist in creating a more realistic assessment of their children's ability and to emphasise to them that their knowledge of the English language was often far from perfect, and that they must take steps to improve it.

Asians on the other hand were often more realistically ambitious and sought higher education.

"Many of the early Asian immigrants in Derby have very able children, particularly the Kenyan Asians. Last year the best two Rolls-Royce apprentices and one of the British Railways Works best first-year apprentices were all Kenyan Asians," the report comments.

It adds that the Youth Employment Officer felt that employers take school leavers entirely on ability whether coloured or not.

White reaction

An approach to ten local firms employing 45,000 people showed that the number of coloured employees was about 1,000. "Nearly every firm reported a favourable reaction from white employees to the employment of coloured people."

The question which provoked the greatest divergence of opinion was: "Do your staff records indicate the country of ethnic origin of employees?"

"Many firms do not have this information and one reply was adamant that records were not kept of the numbers of coloured employees and would regard it as 'shocking' that they should."

Discussion with Derby Trades Union Council representatives confirmed many of the points made by employers. "These revealed a number of real life situations concerning interac-tions of white and coloured staff where common sense by shop stewards and other shop floor men's representatives had cooled down potentially explosive issues."

Limited range

A "murmuring of discontent" from the West Indian community indicated their feeling that only a limited range of jobs were being offered to their school leavers.

"This remark must be taken in the knowledge of the West Indian parents' optimistic opinions on their children's potential and a failure to recognise the imperfections of the West Indians' English language."

The report comments that by some hard work, and a measure of good fortune, Derby had avoided serious disturbances between immigrants and the host community. But if this state of affairs were to be maintained and improved, attention would have to be paid to a number of important factors.

English courses

Employers should be encouraged to run courses in English for Asians and West Indians, not courses in Asian language for English employees, the report contends.

Firms should in their staff records state the country of racial origin of employees, "and special exercises need to be carried out to compare disciplinary measures and promotion applied to coloured staff with similar groups of non-coloureds."

Referring to complaints by immigrants to the Race Relations Board, the report feels that approachable, knowledgeable and well-informed immigrant leaders and Community Relations Officers can clear many of these misunderstandings before a formal complaint is made, if they are asked.

Burning hatred

Turning to the prejudice of white people against coloured people, the report points out that this can range from "mild apprehension at the prospect of being treated by a coloured doctor in a hospital, to a burning hatred of a white worker suspecting that he is going to get the sack because a 'black man' is going to do his job for half the wage."

"These are facts in Derby and again positive steps must be taken to play down the inherent prejudice," the report declares.

"Fortunately, prejudice reduces the greater the white person's education, the younger he is, and the more contact he has with immigrants.

"So the situation looks promising for the future, but will tolerance come quickly enough?"

The first one

"Very careful handling of the first coloured employee is necessary, particularly in smaller firms, to make sure that there is no discrimination to the detriment of white or coloured," says the report.

"Giving a coloured person preference in an attempt to be seen to be more fair to the coloured is equally as bad as giving the white applicant preferential treatment. The first coloured employee must be chosen with extreme care."

The report was directed by Mr. J. E. Lloyd and the project chairman was Mr. J. R. Stables. On the project committee were G. E. Bakewell, A. C. Brewis, R. Cregeen, D. Crowson and L. Oiphin.

WEST INDIAN OFFICIAL'S TRIBUTE TO 'FRIENDLY DERBY'

EVENING TELEGRAPH 3RD DECEMBER 1969

TRIBUTE to the work of Derby West Indian Association was paid at its annual meeting in St. James's Hall by Mr. O. U. Murray, Birmingham divisional officer of the Jamaican High Commission.

Elected to the executive committee were: president, Mr. Charles Hill; vice-president, Mr. M. S. Douglas; secretary, Mr. C. C. McBean; assistant secretary, Mr. Alfred McLean; treasurer, Mr. J. Gordon.

To act under the direction of the executive, a general committee was elected to assist in extending activities and to encourage recruitment of membership.

Mr. Hill reviewed the work of the movement in 1969, and drew attention to several successful dances jointly sponsored by Derby West Indian Association and the International Friendship League.

Emphasising the value of unity he said: "It was most gratifying to observe at our recent Locarno dance the large number of Derby citizens who shared with us the pleasures of that evening."

There was considerable hard work ahead if their plans for progress were to become realities.

Mr. Murray described Derby as "your friendly feeling town." "We of the Jamaican High Commission think well of Derby West Indian Association and the excellent spirit of togetherness you are creating here," he said.

Referring to his recent visit to Jamaica, Mr. Murray stated: "The country is now in the process of improving conditions for everybody. There still remains much to be done, but you may take my word the levelling up of standards of living is well begun."

What West Indians would like to see the CRC doing

36 DERBY EVENING TELEGRAPH, Wednesday, July 20, 1977

WITH reference to recent allegations appearing in the Evening Telegraph directed towards Derby Council for Community Relations, the Derby West Indian Association dissociates itself from attacks on individuals or personalities.

Nevertheless for the Council for Community Relations to be effective, the name should be changed to the proposed name, Derby Council for

Letters . . .

Racial Equality.

Derby West Indian Association would like to see its membership on the executive increased. This would give more voting power.

The West Indian Association expresses its concern for the amount and standard of work done by the CRC. For the CRC to instill confidence in the West Indian population they must strive over the next year to achieve in Derby:

1 An actual monitored programme of equal opportunity in council house allocation.

2 An actual monitored programme of equal opportunity by the 20 large firms in Derby.

3 Under the job creation scheme, more vigorous attempts to involve unemployed West Indian youth.

4 More effective involvement and presence of the professional officers of the CRC.

Derby West Indian Association would like to see me... the str clubs a multi-r

On achieve mean minorit

SOLC Pr

17 Lang Michla

West Indian Association honour blaze hero

FIRE HERO Dennis Dale, who saved two young children from their burning home in May, being presented with a watch by Mr. M. Douglas, secretary of Derby West Indian Association, at his home, 4 Crompton Street, Derby, last night.

Thirteen-year-old Dennis, son of Mr. and Mrs. Eric Dale, dragged Ian Waite (18 months) and his brother, Michael (4), from their smoke-filled home at 5 Crompton Street.

Presenting the watch, Mr. Douglas said: "We think that this little boy has done a really courageous act. For one so young to take such prompt action without regard for his personal safety makes us very proud of him."

Also pictured (from left) are Mr. Charles Hill, president of the association, Mr. Dale, and Mr. J. A. Gordon, vice-president.

Shortly after the rescue, Dennis was taken on a V.I.P. tour of Derby Fire Station, Ascot Drive, and a woman in Kent sent him a £5 cheque for his efforts.

First-class male a VIP

POSTMAN Caleb McBean has won a Post Office award — his third honour for working when his delivery round is over.

For apart from his daily shift, the 64-year-old postie, of Crewe Street, Derby, has a sack-full of roles in the community.

And now the father-of-two has been made a Midland Post Office Personality of the Year for his efforts, along with 13 colleagues from around the region.

They will be invited to a VIP lunch at Birmingham's botanical gardens on February 6, to pick up certificates of merit.

Mr. McBean was a founder member of Derby's West Indian Community Association in 1962 and secured council grants to set-up Carrington Street West Indian Centre.

Married with two sons, he has been a Justice of the Peace since 1982 and deacon of Pear Tree Baptist Church since 1984.

The latest award is the third in six years for Mr McBean, who was given a Jamaican Government badge of honour for his community work in 1985, plus a golden citizen award from the West Indian community last November.

He said: "I don't think the Post Office even knew about the other awards when they put my name forward. I am delighted."

The Midlands head of Post Office public relations, Mike Davis, said: "We know that thousands of our staff work extremely hard supporting organisations in their communities. We thought it time to honour their efforts."

Jamaicans join the Brain Drain for jobs in the sun

DAILY MAIL 3/6/68

By WILLIAM RICHARDS

HUNDREDS of Jamaicans have gone home after obtaining educational qualifications in England.

And the number wanting to re-emigrate has increased 'quite a bit' since Mr Enoch Powell's explosive speech on immigration in Wolverhampton in April.

Each week, dozens of Jamaicans, many skilled but with no qualifications, go to the office of the High Commissioner for Jamaica, looking for jobs.

'By and large, Jamaicans do want to return to Jamaica,' said a spokesman. 'We get dozens of inquiries every week and the number has certainly increased quite a bit since Mr Powell's speech.'

Many firms in Jamaica are encouraging the exodus by advertising top salaries and free air passages to the island in the sun.

Most of the vacancies are for accountants, engineers and doctors.

One of the latest companies encouraging Jamaicans to go home is the Bank of Nova Scotia. It says it has attractive openings for ambitious young men aged 17 to 30, educated to GCE 'O' level or equivalent and for university qualified people suitable for accelerated training to management level.

The bank promises a good salary, pension rights and 'excellent opportunities for advancement.'

Air fares will be paid by the company.

Output

A bank official in Jamaica said: 'We are always on the look out for eligible young men and women.

'Basically, the economy of the island is expanding extremely rapidly. There are opportunities opening up in practically all walks of life.

'We feel the education output of Jamaica is perhaps not as great as required by the economy, although the Government is planning to build 50 secondary schools.'

He added: 'We know there is a large number of Jamaicans and West Indians leaving schools and universities in the United Kingdom this year.'

The High Commission for Jamaica said: 'In most cases the Government, as well as private firms, will pay the employee's fare. He can go either by sea or air.

'Many return because it's their home.'

DERBY EVENING TELEGRAPH, Tuesday, August 5, 1969   23

West Indian among J.P.s sworn in

MUNICIPAL history was made at Derby yesterday when a West Indian, Mr. C. S. Hill, became the town's first coloured magistrate during a swearing-in ceremony at Derby Council House.

Mr. Hill, the president of Derby branch of the West Indian Association, is 48. He came to this country 15 years ago and during almost all of the interim period he has been a printer's assistant with Bemrose and Sons Ltd. at Midland Place.

FOUR MARRIED WOMEN

Yesterday, Mr. Hill was No. 6 among 15 new Derby magistrates, including four married women, who, in turn, before the Mayor of Derby (Alderman Tom Taylor), swore an oath of allegiance to the Queen—also a judicial oath—and declared that they would faithfully and impartially execute their office "according to the best of my judgment and ability."

The new justices include Mr. A. H. Harvey-Bailey, Mr. G. F. Eley, Councillor R. Longdon, Mrs. J. M. Eason, Mrs. D. Tomlinson, Mr. D. E. Redfearn, Dr. V. M. Leveaux, Mr. C. A. Hodgkinson, Mr. J. K. Wareham, Mrs. J. Eldred, Mrs. M. J. Boissier, Mr. T. W. Torney, Mr. W. P. Ward and Mr. A. Thorpe.

They are pictured with the Mayor and Mr. N. S. Fisher, Clerk of the Peace.

Another newly - appointed Derby magistrate, Mrs. Ruth Thompson, a part-time pharmacist at Derbyshire Royal Infirmary, was unable to attend the ceremony for holiday reasons, and will have to be sworn-in later.

Mr. Fisher administered the oaths, and onlookers were led by the Recorder of Derby, Mr. A. W. M. Davies, Q.C., Miss E. M. Grasett (deputising for Mr. F. Peel, chairman, Derby Borough Bench), and Mr. Arthur Exton (Clerk to Derby Borough magistrates).

GOOD FRIEND

Mr. Davies congratulated the new magistrates on their appointments—"you will have great assistance from the experienced magistrates who are already members of the Bench" —and said they would be helped by Mr. Exton, "a hard task-master, but a good friend."

In legal matters the latter would ensure that the newcomers "don't put any feet where they should not be!"

The Recorder added that fortunately, at Derby, the Press did not have an opportunity, because the occasion did not arise, for "printing criticism of the borough magistrates by the Recorder," or vice-versa.

He commented: "I hope that state of affairs will long continue."

Mr. Davies suggested that the new magistrates might spare an hour or two when Derby Borough Quarter Sessions were sitting and sit with him on the Bench.

Except on special occasions they would not be able to adjudicate but, nevertheless, they might find the experience both interesting and helpful.

Fuchsia Society's first show

Mr. D. A. Davison won the cup for the best plant in the show, and the British Fuchsia Society's blue ribbon for the most points, at Derby Fuchsia Society's first show at the Engineers Club, Osmaston Road, Derby.

The cup for the best novices plant was won by Mr. C. Foster.

About 82 entries were judged by the president, Mr. G. Thorley, who is an executive member of the British Fuchsia Society.

'Biggest' bin for Sandiacre litter

Frequently faced with complaints about litter in Sandiacre, the Parish Council had some good news from Councillor W. E. Hart last night.

He said South-East Derbyshire Rural Council were installing the "biggest litter bin he had ever seen" in the Market Place. It cost £40.

PRINCE IN WALES

The Prince of Wales today started a two-day visit to two of the North Wales counties. Denbighshire and Flintshire, as part of his post-investiture "meet the people" tour.

TWO YOUTHS DEALT WITH

School raid—Borstal, suspended sentence

MUSICAL instruments—part of a haul of more than £400 worth of equipment from the Noel-Baker School, Alvaston— were found in an Alvaston house by police officers, Mr. A. R. Arnell, prosecuting, said at Derby Quarter Sessions yesterday.

Other property stolen from the Derby area was also found by Det.-Sgt. J. Reddington and Det.-Con. Frank Newbold.

Two youths involved, Derek Andrew Bernard Bradbury (20), of Gloucester, and Terry Alec Storer (20), of no fixed address, pleaded "Guilty" to entering the Noel-Baker School as trespassers, and stealing musical instruments and equipment worth £406.

Storer also pleaded "Guilty" to entering the office of Aldred's Garage as a trespasser, and stealing a typewriter and a clock, and, with another, entering a store in Brighton Road and stealing cigarettes, tobacco and cigars worth more than £269.

He also admitted taking and driving away a van without the owner's consent, and driving without insurance.

RECENTLY RELEASED

Storer was ordered to be recalled to Borstal and disqualified from driving for a year, and Bradbury was given a six-month prison sentence, suspended for two years.

Mr. Arnell said that both youths had recently been released from Borstal.

Storer had broken into Aldred's Garage, Nightingale Road, and taken a clock and a typewriter after interfering with the safe.

"The office was in a complete state of disorder," commented Mr. Arnell.

Both were involved in breaking into the Noel-Baker School, where they took musical instruments and equipment from the audio and visual language laboratory.

STOLEN VEHICLE

The Brighton Road branch of Derby Co-operative Society was entered through a hole in the ceiling from a conference room.

The cigarettes taken, worth £269, were sold to a man for £100.

A Bedford workabus, stolen in Derby, was used to carry the cigarettes.

Both made statements admitting the offences.

Mr. J. Durman, representing the youths, said that Storer was a lonely person and wanted to move away from Derby, and away from his criminal acquaintances.

Bradbury, he said, had only one previous conviction, for breaking and entering.

COLOURED MAGISTRATE FOR DERBY

DERBY'S first coloured magistrate has been appointed. He is Mr. Charles Sheridan Hill, of 54 Park Grove, Derby, president of Derby Branch of the West Indian Association.

Mr. Hill (48) came to England 15 years ago and has been a printer's assistant at Bemrose and Sons Ltd., Midland Place, Derby, for 14 years.

His wife, Delia, is 50 and they have a son and five daughters.

Mr. Hill is a member of the local committee of the Race Relations Board, the Marriage Guidance Council and the Welfare Committee.

Mr. Hill said today that his appointment was a great honour shared by the vast majority of the migrant community in Derby.

"It is also a tribute to the British people for the traditional sense of justice and fair play for all. This country, and Derby, as a part of it, is a model to the world."

Appointment of other magistrates in page ten.

POLICE CRITICISED IN 'RIOTS' REPORT

DISTURBANCES in Derby last summer were not racially motivated, but many youngsters involved felt frustration caused by feelings of discrimination and harassment by police.

These are the conclusions in the report of Derby Council for Racial Equality's inquiry published today.

Inquiry chairman Mr David Lake

The report contains much criticism of the police handling of the disturbances which it claims were not organised, or primarily racial or "copycat."

It says there was a widespread feeling that the police did little to protect property in the area of Derby largely occupied by minorities.

And it lists grievances against the police which include allegations of racist abuse, harassment, over-enthusiasm by young officers and delays in answering calls from ethnic minority communities.

The inquiry concludes that the disturbances of July 11, 12 and 13 were used by "other forces" in an attempt to drive a wedge between various communities.

There are claims by people caught up in the trouble that police herded people involved to the Pear Tree and Normanton areas of Derby, although this is denied by the police.

The National Front and immigration

O/E/T 24/7/74

IF in voicing the deep seated resentment of many British people to the unwanted influx of coloured immigrants into the UK the National Front is to be accused of racialism, then adequate legal means already exist whereby the Derby Area Trades Union Council sub-committee can voice its complaints.

The NF is a thoroughly democratic national political party, the fourth largest in Britain, whose policy regarding coloured immigration is quiet clear.

The NF is pledged to carry out a policy of phased humane repatriation of all coloured immigrants and their dependents who have entered our country since the passing of the British

Nationality Act of 1948, whereby all citizens of the Commonwealth were declared eligible to regard our country as theirs.

We of the NF seek to revoke this absurd, undemocratic and immoral betrayal of these ideals for which British patriots have died in two world wars.

The people face a stark choice, either Britain for the British, or a multi-racial powder keg.

The NF puts the British first, who does the Trades Union Council sub-committee stand for?

WILLIAM B. MARSON,
Press Officer, National Front, Derby Branch.
15 Langdale Drive, Breadsall.

DERBY EVENING TELEGRAPH, Thursday, November 29, 197

Complacency enemy of community relations

COMPLACENCY is Derby's biggest menace to good community relations, according to the town's Community Relations Officer, Mr George Scott.

Because the inter-communal situation was quiet, we could say that "everything in Derby is lovely," he told a Press conference yesterday.

"This is a very dangerous philosophy, but unfortunately it is held by too many people," he said.

People asked Derby Council for Community Relations (who called the Press conference): "Are you not stirring it up? We do not have a problem."

WARNING

But, warned Mr Scott, Derby was in a full employment situation, and immigration problems did not impinge very much on everyday life.

Whether or not Derby was more or less tolerant than other places had not been tested, but there was "an atmosphere in which we can build."

Much of the credit for the progress that had been made was due to the approach of the local authority, particularly in education, and to the attitude of the police to the community generally.

Referring to employment, Mr Scott said that large local firms appreciated their responsibilities, and made positive efforts towards good relationships.

UNCONSCIOUS

But there were other firms who were "completely unconscious of the problem."

Mr Scott said that when he began work six years ago he had a hard job getting co-operation from landlords and building societies over accommodation for immigrants. There had been a big improvement, but there was still one building society that were unco-operative.

Mr J. A. Smith, West Indian representative on the council, recalled that 16 years ago, when he was in the RAF and stationed in Derby, he had not found Derby more tolerant than other places.

He had had difficulty in getting lodgings, the reaction of landladies being: "What would my white lodgers think?" or "What would the neighbours think?"

Even the YMCA had discouraged him from playing badminton there, and he had

gone to Nottingham to play.

"I certainly think that we cannot be too complacent," he said.

In his report to the conference, Mr Scott said that a programme of lectures and discussion groups had developed in some 40 schools and colleges throughout Derby and Derbyshire, serviced by members and officers of Community Relations Councils.

"Derby holds a unique position in multi-racial education and language training," he said.

"We see the re-education of the host community, particularly the younger generation, as our highest priority."

RE-STRUCTURED

"Minority groups as a whole, however, must realise their responsibility for playing a much more active part in this process of integration than they do at present, he said.

Mr J. R. Stables, chairman of the employment sub-committee, in a report said that "many people see no potential problem in introducing immigrant workers into employment.

"Yet any change like introducing the first coloured worker into a firm or the promotion of the first coloured foreman, can explode any weaknesses in a firm's induction, training or promotional systems."

Mr Stables said that when firms had tackled their problems positively and imaginatively, racial integration had not proved difficult to achieve.

The report of the housing sub-committee, the chairman of which is Mr W. R. Thompson, said that a comprehensive file of information, regularly updated was being compiled.

It had been agreed that when areas of minority groups were affected by redevelopment schemes, members of the sub-committee would be prepared to meet groups to explain the

---

Community group seek information

30/11/74

DISCUSSIONS over a proposed weekend conference with teenagers from other towns and cities were postponed by Derby Junior Council for Community Relations.

The council decided that before they arrange the conference to discuss social and community problems, they should go to similar conferences held by stronger and long established councils.

It was agreed to hold an international evening which will be open to any musical group who would like to play, and before that, a Caribbean evening to integrate West Indians into the functions of the council.

Mrs G. Gamble, a member of the Senior Council for Community Relations, reported on the state of the social and cultural sub-committee, of which she is chairman and with which the junior council helps.

She said that there were various schemes and ideas ready to be discussed in committee and thanked the junior council for their assistance in social and cultural events.

Chairman, Mr F. Hartropp, told the council that the senior council had asked for contributions for a regular newsletter.

Conception of the Derby West Indian Community Association

The Derby West Indian Community Association (DWICA) is widely believed to be one of the oldest organisations of its kind in the UK, having evolved out of a desire to provide support for the local community back in 1955. This chapter of the DWICA story is further illuminated by the minutes preserved from the time, as well as the information gathered for a special exhibition to celebrate the association's sixtieth anniversary held in 2017.

This journey from a fledgling association features the people who were instrumental in its formation, the decisions made and the events that were organised or attended by its members.

1955

In 1955, members of the African Caribbean community in Derby came together to create an organised group that would work towards addressing social and welfare issues in their community. These individuals, who had the necessary skills and were committed to the cause, wanted to find a positive way to communicate these issues to other organisations such as the police and Derby City Council.

Early meetings were held in members' homes in the Pear Tree and Normanton area of Derby and were attended by both men and women in the evenings. Unfortunately, there is no written evidence of the activities and efforts of the African Caribbean community at that time. However, the group's aim was to not only support the community, but to also sustain it for future generations.

1961

After months of meetings and discussions, the first public meeting of the Derby West Indian Association (DWIA) was held at St James Church Hall on Dairyhouse Road on the 31st October 1961. Guests were welcomed by the chairman, Mr Ray Jones, who was the guest speaker for the evening and discussed the importance of education.

Two months later, on the 2nd December, the members held a meeting at the Normanton Hotel to officially form the organisation. Mr

West Indians in Derby form an association

DERBY West Indian Association was formed at a meeting at Normanton Hotel, Derby, attended by 50 people.

A draft constitution was approved and the following officers were elected: President, Dr. C. Meade, West Hallam; vice-president, Mr. C. Hill, Derby; secretary, Mr. M. S. Douglas, Derby; assistant secretary, Mr. R. Barnes, Derby; treasurer, Mr. C. McBean, Derby.

"GOOD AUGURY"

Mr. A. L. Bethune, an officer of the West Indies Commission in London, was the guest speaker. He congratulated the group on the broad lines of the constitution, and said he felt it was a "good augury to improve relations with our English friends."

This was the goal the West Indian Government envisaged for West Indians who had settled in the United Kingdom, he said.

Mr. C. Hill presided.

Charles Hill presided over the gathering which was attended by one hundred people, leading to their acceptance of the constitution after some minor revisions. At the same meeting, officers were elected and the name of the association was adopted.

The officers elected were: Dr CE Meade (President), Mr Charles Hill (Vice-President), Mr Caleb McBean (Treasurer), Mr Sheridan Douglas (Secretary) and Mr R Barnes (Vice-Secretary). Furthermore, 12 committee members were elected at the gathering: J Smith, P Riley, Mrs Channer, Mr Channer, Mr GA Powell, C Brooks, Mrs P Hutchinson, G Francis, G Davidson, Mr Stanley, A Cowell and G Rochester.

The elections were supported by Mr A Bethune, the Community Development Officer from the Migrant Services Department located in London.

The members of the DWIA recognised the importance of attending national events and, at their meeting on the 9th of December at the Normanton Hotel, agreed that one of their members should attend the Migrant Services Conference in London on the 16th of December. Mr Douglas volunteered for the role and members donated money for his expenses. However, the conference was later postponed to February 1962, so the donations were returned.

1962

On 18th January 1962, members of DWIA gathered at 25 Crewe Street, the home of the Treasurer Mr McBean. At this meeting, the members wrote a letter to the Derby Town Clerk requesting the creation of a West Indian Liaison Officer to work not only with the West Indian community, but with people from other Commonwealth countries.

At the meeting on 15th February 1962, the DWIA discussed the contents of a letter from the Derby City Council about the recruitment of a West Indian Liaison Officer. They agreed to set up a selection committee to look at the recruitment process, and also decided to postpone the annual Federation Dance from 15th June to 3rd August, which coincided with Jamaica's first anniversary of Independence. A committee was set up for arranging the dance and other celebrations, and its members were Mr Hill, Dr Meade, Mr McDonald, Mr McBean, Mr Barnes, Miss Chambers and Mr Douglas. It was agreed that from then onwards the Federation Dance would be referred to as the Jamaica Independence Dance.

At the meeting on 30th March 1962, held at the Cambridge Hotel, it was noted that the Derby Town Clerk had requested more information on the role of West Indian Liaison Officer. The DWIA agreed to reply with a letter asking for clarification on progress with the role. A letter from the Secretary of the Migrant Services Division was shared, confirming his attendance to a DWIA meeting to speak on the Commonwealth Immigrants Bill. The suggested date was 27th April 1962.

Mr J Scott, the Warden of Ventures Youth Club, also spoke to members about the history of youth clubs in England and invited two volunteers from the DWIA to be trained as youth leaders. If the volunteers showed significant aptitude, they were offered the opportunity to attend a residential training centre, where they could gain a National Certificate for their efforts. This, it was felt, could be crucial in building relationships between the youth and the community.

On 5 May 1962, the DWIA discussed opening their first bank account with Midland Bank (now HSBC) on Normanton Road. At the Cambridge Hotel, the Vice President gave a brief report to members at a meeting on 25 May, where details were shared from a meeting held on 27 April at the Derby Guildhall.

In July and August 1962, two meetings were held at the Normanton Hotel. At the first, on 30 July, the final arrangements for the Jamaica Independence Dance were discussed, which was to be held on 3 August at the Locarno Ballroom on Babington Road. It was suggested that a local band would play at the dance, but it was deemed that the time-scale was too short and the application was denied. However, the DWIA offered to help publicise the band's future events.

At the second meeting, held on 18 August, the DWIA discussed the success of the Jamaica Independence Dance, which the treasurer noted as being the first big event undertaken by the organisation. The success was attributed to the volunteers who contributed, who were duly thanked. It was agreed at this meeting that the Jamaica Independence Dance would become an annual event. Demonstrating excellent organisational skills, the Secretary was given the mandate to find a venue for the next event to take place in August the following year.

On the 25th of August 1962, the first of several meetings between the DWIA and St James's Church Hall was held. Sir Learie Constantine, Trinidad and Tobago's High Commissioner to the UK and former West Indies cricketer, sent a message of introduction which was received by the DWIA. In response, it was agreed that an invitation be extended for him to visit and arrangements for the use of St James' Church Hall were suggested. At this meeting, the DWIA confirmed that the second Jamaica Independence Dance would be an annual event, and discussed plans for the annual children's party.

The relationship between St James' Church and the DWIA was further cemented when, on the 29th September 1962, the reverend addressed members about apartheid in South Africa. Meetings at St James' Church Hall continued right up until 1968. On the 27th

October 1962, Mr Fitzpatrick, a journalist and DWIA member, gave a presentation on world affairs. This exemplified the DWIA's mission to not only meet the needs of the West Indian community, but to also look for ways to help the community as a whole.

On the 24th November 1962, the DWIA held its first Annual General Meeting at St James' Church Hall. The proceedings of the AGM, presided over by Mr N McCarthy, included the presentation of the annual report as well as the election of officers and committee members.

The new DWIA executive team included Mr RC Barnes, who was elected as President, Mr CS Hill as Vice President, Mr C McBean as Treasurer, and Mr MS Douglas and Miss AJ Martin as Secretary and Assistant Secretary, respectively. Committee members elected included Mr BR Ramsay, Mr G Powell, Mr G Davidson, Mr V Sewell, Mrs M Case, Mr W Smith, Mr K Dennis, Mr H South, Mr P Riley, Mr HE Emanuel, Mr JA Scott and Mr G Francis.

At the following meeting, held at the Normanton Hotel in December the same year, President Barnes welcomed the new members and encouraged them to contribute to the success of the DWIA. This included familiarising themselves with the constitution and draft rules, which were to be discussed in a future meeting. It was also unanimously decided at this meeting that a dance should be held at a later date to raise funds for a children's party.

The 29th December saw the DWIA gather again at the St James' Church Hall. On this occasion, President Barnes thanked all the volunteers that had helped make the dance, held on the 22nd December, a success. The guest speaker, Mr A Bethune from the Jamaican Migrant Services Office in London, gave a talk entitled 'Greater Unity Amongst the West Indians', which sparked a discussion and appreciation for the progress that DWIA had made.

1963

At the beginning of 1963, the DWIA held its first meeting on the 9th February at 159 Sale Street. During this meeting, the committee members were presented with two letters: one from Mr Bethune expressing his gratitude to the DWIA for the courteous reception he received during his last visit, and another from Flamingo regarding the promotion of a dance competition set to take place in Derby. The committee was in favour of the competition, but as there was not enough time, they decided to go ahead with the competition on the 15th April and to host a parents' meeting with Mr Phelps, the Youth Employment Officer, as their guest speaker.

On the 23rd of February, Mr Phelps attended the meeting at St James' Church hall and gave a presentation on young people leaving school and the Youth Employment Service. He explained how each child had the opportunity to use this service before they departed from school, and provided valuable one-on-one advice during the Q&A session. Parents found this talk to be both informative and helpful in understanding exactly what young people may need in order to reach their desired goals.

Finally, Mrs Webster from the social services attended the meeting on the 30th March at the same church hall and gave a presentation on the formation of a women's section within the DWIA. She offered her help in making sure that the venture was successful, and nominated and seconded Mrs Shelia Barnes to be acting Secretary. At the end of the meeting, Mr Frank Salesbury put on an entertaining magic show, which was reported to be brilliant. This event showed the respect that the community had for the DWIA, and how it could influence activities and events in Derby for both the West Indian and wider community.

At the DWIA meeting on the 9th April 1963, the annual summer trips were confirmed. On the 2nd June, the group would be travelling to Llandudno in Wales, with the fare set at 20 shillings. On the 4th August, the group would be travelling to Skegness, a seaside town in Lincolnshire, with the fare set at 21/6 shillings. Concessions were agreed upon, including the decision that children aged five to seven could travel for free, with a second child travelling with a single parent being charged half price.

At this same meeting, petty cash of 10 shillings was approved to be given to the Secretary for use on stationery items such as stamps and phone calls. Members were also informed of an upcoming meeting of the ladies' section of the DWIA on the 30th April, to which the DWIA would be covering their expenses.

The members of DWIA also praised two ladies from the group for their positive representation in the community. So highly thought of were these women that Mr Hill suggested the Association write letters of thanks and appreciation to them. In the minutes, these ladies were said to have "done extremely well" and to have "served the Association so well".

At the 11th May 1963 meeting, members showed great enthusiasm for the upcoming trip to Llandudno on Sunday 2nd June. They had seen enquiries and tickets sold, and began discussing the Annual Jamaica Independence Dance, to be held on 2nd August. It was agreed that the entrance fee would be 5 shillings and local dignitaries such as the Lord Mayor, Mayoress and the Jamaica High Commissioner would be invited.

Mr A Bethune attended the meeting, and suggested that quarterly financial statements be shared with members at each meeting in order to keep them informed of the Association's progress. Everyone present agreed that this should be a regular item at future meetings.

In addition to reading the minutes, the Association invited a number of guest visitors to meetings throughout 1963. These included people from the local community, as well as representatives from organisations within and outside Derby.

On the 25th May 1963, Mr Hawthorne was invited to the meeting as the guest speaker. His presentation included a slideshow featuring different conferences and meetings from all around the world and was focused on the 'moral rearmament as related to the brotherhood of man'. After Mr Hawthorne's presentation, Mr Dick Duce led a question and answer session. All in attendance thanked the two speakers for their presentation, and the President of the meeting noted that the level of interest and enthusiasm was high, hoping that it would continue.

The following week, on the 8th of June, another social event was held with Mr Eric Irons as the guest speaker. He was particularly fortunate to have been in Jamaica for the country's 1962 Independence and shared stories and photographs outlining the cultural, industrial and economic changes taking place there. He also mentioned the various training schemes created to up-skill young Jamaicans, leading to the country's rapid development over the last few years. Following Mr Irons' presentation, he took part in a question and answer session. The members thanked him for sharing his knowledge and experiences and wished him luck in his new role as a magistrate.

At the meeting of 22nd June, the High Commissioner of Jamaica shared a letter expressing his regret that he would be unable to attend the Jamaican Independence Dance, which was due to take place on 2nd August. However, he promised to send a representative in his stead. Additionally, a letter of thanks was shared from Mr Hawthorne in reference to his attendance at the meeting of 25th May. Miss M Kelly was chosen to represent the organisation at the Conservative Coffee Club.

In relation to the Skegness trip, which was planned for 4th August, it was suggested by Mr Hill that a new destination be chosen. The minutes do not mention the reason for the change of plans, but it was agreed that Mr M Parkin should be informed of the new arrangement, including the new departure time and coach quotes. Lastly, a letter was sent to the West Indies Cricket Club to promote the need for unity.

At the meeting on 13th July, at St. James' Church Hall, the promotion manager of the Flamingo and the president of the Derbyshire Netball Team had their letters read out and were both received warmly. It was decided that the film unit from the Flamingo should be invited to film at DWIA on 28th September. Additionally, two committee members were to attend a dinner in honour of the Jamaican Netball Team, and as a thank you, Mrs Guthrie was given a complimentary ticket in recognition of her hard work and dedication on the DWIA's Women's section.

At the next meeting a week later, on 29th July, letters from the High Commissioner's Office and the Standing Conference of West Indies were shared. The committee voted to support two DWIA members to attend a charity cricket match at the Oval Cricket Ground in London on 14th September. They then discussed the possibility of acquiring a copy of the message from Jamaica's Prime Minister, Alexander Bustamante, on Jamaica's Independence on 6th August 1962.

At the meeting held on September 14th, 1963, which took place at St. James' Church hall, a letter was read discussing the potential promotion of the well-known Flamingo magazine. This magazine was allegedly used to spread the anti-communist message, and its primary audience was people from the West Indian community. Members were then asked if they would like to offer their services as canvassers.

The meeting also agreed that any individuals who were ill in the community should have their condition shared within the group, and members would make sure to visit them.

On January 28th, 1963, a special meeting was held at 25 Crewe Street to decide the plans for the upcoming event for the members. A dinner and dance was to be held at the Friary Hotel on October 31st, and a sum of £50 was allocated for the event.

On the 5th of November, 1963, St. James Church hosted a highly-anticipated social entertainment evening for members in conjunction with Flamingo Magazine, who provided promotional material. Ken Campbell, Flamingo's promotions manager, was particularly impressed with the turnout of attendees and revealed that this was the largest he had ever seen. As a result, the meeting concluded with all present agreeing to the proceeds of the upcoming fundraising dance on the 7th of December be used to help fund a Children's Christmas Party. Only paid members were allowed to vote at the Annual General Meeting held on the 30th of November.

Mr A. Bethume, the officer for the Jamaica High Commission, acted as chairperson for the third AGM, with Mr RC Barnes as President, Mr CS Hill as Vice-President, Mr C McBean as Treasurer, Mr MS Douglas as Secretary, and Miss AJ Martin as Assistant Secretary. Other members of the committee included Mr D Davison, Mr H South, Mr C Hill, Mr Barnes, Mr B Ramsey, Mr J Scott, Miss N Rhule, Mr H Samuel, Mr V Sewell, and Mr N Braham. Mr Wint resigned.

The AGM was further distinguished by the presence of Wilson Hill, a Jamaican Senator, and Felix Taylor, a Parliamentary Secretary in the Ministry of Local Government. They presented on the proposed investigation into the living conditions of Jamaican nationals in Britain, and continued with a question and answer session on Jamaican education.

On 16 December, an emergency meeting was convened for the executive members to discuss amending a clause in their constitution. After lengthy conversations, four revisions were made. On 21 December, the committee agreed to bear the full costs of the annual children's party that had been held on December 12.

1964

The first meeting of the year was held on 25th January and was a social event, at which approximately 150 people watched the film 'A Nation is Born'. At a meeting on 27th February, the committee organised an outing to London on 17th May. This was a departure from the usual seaside trips and the agreed price was 24 shillings for adults and half price for children.

DWIA was committed to the community and their events were open to members, their families and the wider community, demonstrating the importance of community cohesion. This ethos is still seen today in events and their support of other organisations in and outside of Derby.

At the meeting on 28 March, members discussed and arranged a great social event to be held on 6 June. This event included a film session on the Jamaican independence of 1962, and the annual Independence Dance on August 7th featuring a steelband. Admission was set at six shillings, and the Jamaica High Commissioner was invited. On 25 April, members and friends gathered to watch 'Sunshine Beards'.

Normal meetings resumed on 30 May, where the guest speaker, Miss Clay from the Marriage Guidance Council, gave a presentation on their activities and role in marriage counselling. At the meeting on 27 June, members requested that minutes from the previous meetings be available at the start of the meeting. Nowadays, minutes are typically presented to members ahead of the meeting for their review and validation.

At the next meeting, held on April 7th, members decided to form a youth organisation. St. James' Church kindly offered the use of their hall for the foreseeable future, and a letter from Miss Rhule, a worker from the Oxfam Group, was read. In the letter, Miss Rhule proposed

The DWICA Logo

Keen observers may note that the logo design for the Derby West Indian Community Association reflects some elements within the crest adopted by the West Indies cricket team. The team itself is seen as a unifying force both within the Caribbean region and the diaspora. During the 1960s and 1970s, the West Indies cricket team was heading towards the pinnacle of its dominance of the sport. DWICA, therefore, paid its own tribute by emulating certain aspects within the crest's design. The organisation's motto, "We Unite To Achieve", further reflects the sense of unity among Derby's Caribbean community and Caribbean people across the United Kingdom.

exploring the possibility of working in partnership sometime in the future.

Miss Pat Douce was the guest at the meeting of July 25th. She presented the members with photographs of her uncle, Ernest Shackleton's Antarctic expeditions and the members reportedly enjoyed it. They were very engaged during the question and answer session that followed.

The final two meetings of the year took place on 19th August and 28th November at two separate venues: 59 Sale Street and St James' Church. On both occasions, the members discussed the annual children's Christmas party, which was prompted by the group's commitment to their community and was open to any child free of charge. 'Santa' would appear and each child would receive a gift.

Unfortunately, due to a lack of attendance, the AGM in November was postponed until the 30th January 1965. However, the executive officers decided to remain in their positions and to continue with their usual duties until the members could vote in a new executive team in January.

In the 1960s, the Derby Women's Institute Committee (DWIC) only held twelve meetings, compared with the previous decade. Most meetings were hosted at St James Church. Unfortunately, there is no evidence to suggest why the meetings dwindled and records are sparse.

The Community Building

As the Derby Caribbean community grew in the 1950s, so did the membership of the Derby West Indian Association (DWIA). To support the Association's various duties and responsibilities, its members agreed in December 1968 that committees should be formed for social events, welfare, general purposes, and outings. Meetings were held in the homes of members and at various other locations, such as St James' Church Hall, Pear Tree House, Normanton Hotel, Cambridge Hotel and Hodgkinson Coffee Bar.

In the early 1970s, it was becoming clear that the Association needed a building of its own to cater for the needs of the local Caribbean community. In the first instance, the provision of a day centre was a top priority.

West Indians find site for centre

THE three-year-old hope for a community centre for Derby West Indians which has faced many setbacks has progressed to the point of finding a site

The city council have agreed to sell land in Carrington Street to Derby West Indian Association for nearly £10,000

But the original grant aid of £49,000 has been eroded says assistant chief executive Mr Ray Cowlishaw in a report Even a medium-sized building is impossible. with the land purchase

The association are asking the council to give them the £10,000

The policy and resources committee will decide on Wednesday

Evening Telegraph

On 28th August 1975, the Management Committee resolved to put together a working group and look into building ownership. Further discussions on 4th September 1976, decided that the day centre was to provide a hall to accommodate 200 people, a nursery, a room for the elderly West Indians, a library, committee room, and a range of furniture and indoor games equipment. Though the Association lacked the required funds, it was decided to secure an urban aid grant and apply for government funding to turn their vision into a reality.

With this, DWIA committed to working hard to secure a community building and by investing efforts, time and resources, the organisation was able to manifest their long-term goal.

Early in his DWIA presidency in 1977, Mr Solomon 'Ricky' Walters made a commitment to the membership to establish a community facility for members of the local Caribbean population.

Working with Derby Council for Voluntary Services, an application was made to the Department of the Environment for a grant towards a 'Day Centre', with a hall to provide accommodation for 200 people, a nursery, a room for the elderly West Indians, a library, office, Committee Room, indoor games equipment and furnishings. However, the application was unsuccessful.

With the help of Race Equality Council (REC) Chief Officer, Janet Fletcher Davis, DWIA submitted a successful bid in the fiscal year

METHODS OF PAYMENT

Nº 3968

(i) Directly into the Centre Fund
     Raising Account: No. 91026208
     MIDLAND BANK LIMITED,
     91026208 D.W.I.A. CENTRE A/C.
     216 NORMANTON ROAD,
     DERBY. DE3 6WB

(ii) Direct to the D.W.I.A.
     by posting to :-
          MR. C.C. McBEAN,
          HON.SECRETARY,
          25 CREWE STREET,
          DERBY.
               Telephone: 31497
     If you require a receipt please tick box :

     [ ] Yes   [ ] No

(iii) By giving to an Authorised Collector
      OUR RECEIPT

I, Mr/Ms/Mrs.........................
                              Collector
received the sum of £.........
from Mr/Ms/Mrs......................
                              Contributor
       on......................(Date)
SIGNED...............................
                              Collector
SIGNED...............................

YOUR RECEIPT

Nº 3968

I Mr/Ms/Mrs.........................
                    (Authorised Collector)
received the sum of £....................
from Mr/Ms/Mrs......................
                         (Contributor)
on................(date) in respect of
Scheme.

          Tick Box

     [1]   [2]

SIGNED...............................
     (Collector)

SIGNED...............................
     (Contributor)

PUBLICITY
**Names of All Contributors
and Progress of the Fund to be
announced in the
D.W.I.A. News Letters**

Fund Raising Scheme
WEST INDIAN
Community & Culture
CENTRE

THE PROJECT

To build a West Indian Community /
Cultural Centre in Derby.

We have now acquired a plot of land
on Carrington Street on which to build a
NEW CENTRE.   Plans have been drawn up and
building work is scheduled to begin in
March, 1981.

WHY A CENTRE?

This much needed Centre will be your
Centre and will stand as a monument, not
only for ourselves, but for our children
and grandchildren.   A Centre that will
meet the needs of our community from the
very young to the very old, so we are
convinced that you will wish to support
this exciting venture.

YES! YOU CAN HELP

It is estimated that the whole project
(Phase 1 and Phase 2) will cost £250,000
The Urban Aid Grant that we received some
time ago was for a considerable amount
less than that - £49,000 in fact.   So,
you can see that we still have a long way
to go, but, if we can raise £25,000 now
then we shall be able to complete
Phase 1 in 1981, so, your help is vital.
Why not buy your first brick NOW!

OUTLINE OF FUND-RAISING SCHEMES

(1)   BUY-A-BRICK SCHEME

A direct contribution of a minimum of
£5.00 towards the Project.   A unit of £5.00
or multiple will buy you one or more bricks
for the Centre and entitle you to have your
name recorded on a plaque for posterity, to
be permanently displayed in the Centre.

(2)   OPEN DONATION SCHEME

A direct contribution of any lesser
sum is acceptable.   This scheme does not
entitle you to have your name inscribed
on the plaque.

ACTION TIME

Let's get down to the nitty gritty!
We are sure you will wish to buy a brick
straight away.

In demonstrating your support, we
invite you to complete the attached
form opposite.

THE COMMUNITY
NEEDS
YOUR SUPPORT
N O W !

****

OUTLINE OF FUND-RAISING SCHEMES

(1)   BUY-A-BRICK SCHEME

Contributions of £5.00 units or
multiples entitles you to have your name
inscribed on a plaque in the Centre.

(2)   OPEN DONATION SCHEME

Donations of any lesser amount but
not entitling you to have your name
inscribed on a Centre plaque.

CONTRIBUTOR

NAME.................................
ADDRESS.............................
....
POST CODE............Tele............

I wish to participate in Scheme No:-

     [1]   [2]

Tick as applicable.

See overleaf for further details.

1977/78 under the Home Office's Urban Aid programme through Derbyshire County Council.

Finding the land on which to build the community facility proved to be a challenge. Following the intervention of Milton Crosdale OBE, as the new REC Chief Officer, and working in partnership with the DWIA President, the land for the community building was secured. The first phase of the building project began in 1981.

Soon after phase one was built, DWIA was presented an opportunity as a result of a failed Urban Aid project that left £100 000 spare. Milton Crosdale was approached by the funders to discuss with DWIA the opportunity and the benefit it would bring to the community. There was a short time, 24hrs, to respond to the invitation which meant DWIA called an emergency meeting, and it was agreed to accept the funding. DWIA then commissioned builders to build to specification a large hall for community events (Phase 2, the main hall).

Cuts hit centre scheme

A scheme for a community centre for the Derby West Indian Association may be held up by Government economy cuts.

The plan has been approved by the council's education committee and a sum of £59,000 earmarked for capital and running costs

But now it has been deferred for reconsideration in the autumn

Mr. Caleb McBean, secretary of the association, which has 400 members, said he hoped this would not mean a long delay. They were looking at a site in Castle Ward, offered by the city council, and were hoping for an early agreement.

The build took approximately a year to complete and the DWIA community / Cultural Centre was officially opened on 31st July 1982, jointly, by the Mayor of Derby, Councillor Norman Glen and the Lord Lieutenant of Derbyshire, Sir Peter Hilton. The High Commissioner of Trinidad and Tobago, Eustace Seigaret, was the guest of honour.

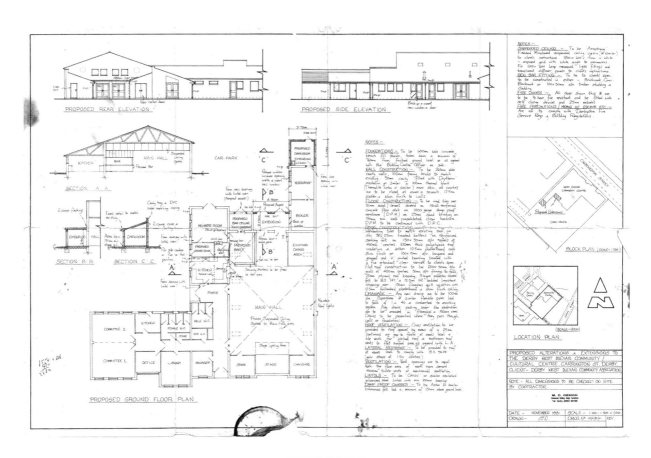

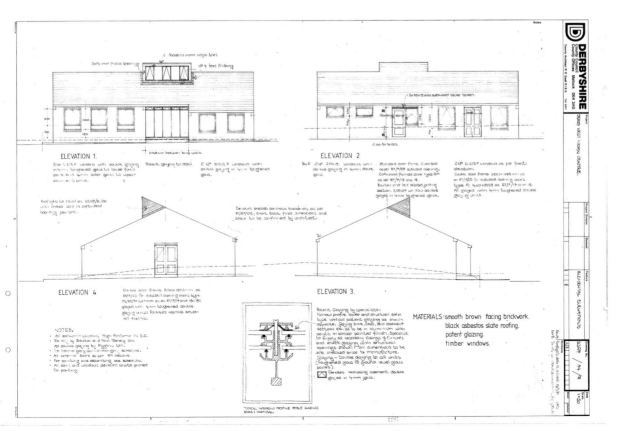

The ribbon-cutting ceremony finally established a community facility for the African Caribbean community living in Derby and surrounding areas. Since 1982, the centre has been the hub for many of Derby's African Caribbean community.

Since 1982, flagship projects like the Summer School and the Derby Caribbean Carnival continue today, and other community organisations have grown from it, such as the Hadhari Project whose Burton Road building supports elders in the city.

As part of DWIA's further development, it was agreed that the Association should seek 'charitable status'. The organisation completed a registration process which resulted in DWIA amending its name with the inclusion of word 'Community'. On the 17th December 1985, the Association obtained charitable status and would hence be known as Derby West Indian Community Association (DWICA). It is registered with the Charity Commission for England and Wales, registration number 517068.

DWICA still operates services from its community centre on Carrington Street, therefore making it one of the oldest African Caribbean community organisations in the UK.

Acknowledgements are due to the following people who worked tirelessly to help establish the Derby West Indian Community Cultural Centre: Mr S.A. Walters (DWIA President); Mr Charles White; Mr Brian Ambrose; Mr Scott; Mr Humpston; Mr Taylor; Mr Calladine; Mr Milton Crosdale (Council for Racial Equality); Mr Mick Walker (Derby City Councillor); Mr Ray Cowlishaw (Derby City Council – CEO); Mr Sam Lee; Mr C McBean; Mr G Mighty; Mr Bob Laxton (Derby City Council Leader); Mr Roy Fraser; Mr Gordon; Miss N. Hudson; Mr R. Barnes; Mr Douglas.

Building Timeline

Below gives a detailed summary breakdown of the process, barriers, opportunities and dynamics undertaken by DWIA to establish DWIA community / cultural centre.

11.12.76 DWIA Management committee meeting at Pear Tree House

DWIA Urban aid grant – This application was based costs on establishing a day centre, at that time it was £40 000 (£273 057 today 2022). Members discussed in detail. The Chairman & Secretary were scheduled to meet Mr John Griffiths who was going to support the bid but needed some practical management solutions as to how DWIA could sustain the building if it was given.

Members agreed to membership fee for the centre should be around £2.00 (£13.65 today 2022) overall, A Covenant Scheme for raising funds, a fundraising committee be set up and a gift shop. Members also agreed the centre would be staffed by volunteers in the main which included the management committee.

Early stages of construction of the community/cultural centre

29.1.77 DWIA Management committee meeting at Pear Tree House

The Urban Aid grant application was read out to members for a capital expenditure project to establish a day centre. Members agreed that whether the application was approved this year or not that DWIA fundraising for the day centre should be put in motion

Letter from Council for Community Equality confirmed DWIA urban aid grant application would be put forward to the Council's Finance and General-Purpose Committee.

2.4.77 DWIA Management committee Special meeting at Pear Tree House

The process of re-applying for urban aid for the post was revisited by the committee and discussed by members in a reply from the council who suggested DWIA could apply again this year for a grant however needed to choose between the youth and community worker post or the day care centre. It was agreed to discuss

at a members meeting and consideration should be given to DWIA future developments

23.4.77 DWIA Annual General Meeting (AGM) at Pear Tree House

As part of the AGM process the Secretary guided members through their report which was accepted and approved by the membership and the highlight being his recommendation to re-apply to urban aid for funds to establish a day centre as this would be of benefit for all West Indians in Derby

8.8.77 DWIA Emergency committee meeting at Havana Night Club

Committee members discussed at great length and as a result agreed to re-submit new funding application for the youth & community post and submit a new application for the West Indian cultural centre.

Community/cultural centre under construction and, right, well on the way to completion

13.8.77 DWIA membership meeting at Pear Tree House

Members agreed to support the committee to re-apply for a grant to fund the youth & community post and a new application for the Day Centre.

The Chairman informed members that the Covenant Scheme would be operational soon as well as a suitable location found for the charity shop. In addition, a number of subcommittees were now in place to deal with DWIA activities and management. It was also mentioned that a carnival committee should be considered.

11.10.77 Committee meeting at Pear Tree House

Letter from Derbyshire County Council acknowledging DWIA request to re-submit application for youth and community post and a representative from the urban aid working party would like to discuss in detail the day centre application.

26.11.77 DWIA Members meeting at Pear Tree House

The Treasurer presented a plan to raise funds for the day centre. Members present were given a copy of the covenant that would be developed for fundraising. The Covenant Scheme was considered as a practical scheme and members should approve it once it had all the relevant details included. In addition, it was mentioned that a building on Burton Road was up for sale at £45,000 which was considered as suitable for DWIA to carry out different projects. A member from the floor suggested DWIA seek financial support from other bodies as a backup if the urban aid bid was not successful

11.2.78 committee meeting at Pear Tree House

Derbyshire County Council letter confirmed DWIA application to the Department of the Environment would be put forward with the backing/support of the council. Members discussed the long term aims and objects of the proposed DWIA day centre and assurances confirmed that if established the centre would serve the whole West Indian community

1.7.78 DWIA Members meeting at Pear Tree House

Correspondences

Derbyshire County Council letter - stating DWIA funding application to the Department of the Environment was successful and the County Council will honour its financial contribution as detailed in the bid.

CRE letter - giving advice on seeking more help for the day centre building project and congratulating DWIA on winning the grant.

Members were brought up to date with the **Urban Aid funding bid** from the Department of the Environment regarding DWIA day centre. The Secretary suggested a sub-committee should be set up to negotiate with Derbyshire County Council

Members agreed that DWIA committee should meet on 9th July to discuss and agree a negotiation team to lead on the project with Derbyshire County Council who wanted to meet DWIA during July

9.7.78 DWIA Management committee Special meeting at The Havana Night club

Negotiation team established as DWIA Chairman, Secretary, Treasurer, Mr Davidson and Mr Mighty. It was agreed to ask Mr Wint to be a member of the team. Suggested dates for the meeting with D/shire County Council were Monday 17th or Tuesday 25th July and the Chairman of the CRE should be invited to the meeting

13.8.78 DWIA Management committee Special meeting at The Havana Night club

DWIA Treasurer stated the Building **Covenant Scheme** was pushed back in order to assess in detail which option is best suited for DWIA (a free donation or a charitable arrangement) members agreed to a voluntary agreement to start with. The Chairman suggested the Treasurer have a workable scheme in place by Feb 1979

The Secretary gave members a full report on the meeting with the County Council regarding the Urban Aid Grant on the following points:

• the building
• management and running costs
• wardens' terms of reference

• the next step - that a meeting to have a detailed look at Unity Hall took place on Monday 31st July 1978 10.00am.

Mr Ambrose listed further points that required further investigation e.g. Public liability requirements, fire escape, to check stair case regulations. To take action in respect of basement, to check the electrical system. Mr Ambrose informed the committee that all checks and investigations to be undertaken would be an expense to DWIA if it pursued the **Unity Hall** option. Members agreed to wait for the architect's report on the building before making any decisions

16.9.78 DWIA Members meeting at Pear Tree House

Urban Aid update – From research work undertaken the Secretary reported that the Unity Hall was not a viable centre based on renovation and repair costs. It was agreed to find another building option

The DWIA Subcommittee set up to work with Derbyshire County Council suggested it needed support from professionals in the construction industry in order to make the best use of the grant. It was agreed that an advisory group made up of professionals should be established

28.1.79 DWIA Management committee meeting at The Havana Night club

Urban Aid update – DWIA Secretary duly gave the following update on the Day centre – work is still ongoing to find a suitable location, St Augustine Church on Almond Street may be selling their church hall which could be considered. In addition, Derby City Council is to confirm if DWIA can opt for a site to build a centre.

Mr Lee confirmed he and other sub-committee members were still working on the building Covenant Scheme

Closing stages of construction of the community/cultural centre

As part of the research process to obtain a building for the Association members discussed the option put forward by Mr Gabbidon for the purchase of Pear Tree House. Members discussed the option and concluded that it was not likely for the building to become available, and the building was considered to be too small

25.2.79 DWIA Management committee meeting at The Havana Night

Covenant Scheme - Mr Lee confirmed that work is still ongoing and as a result of talking to the members a possible template could be established to implement the scheme and collecting cash from members. The next development process would be to confirm the fixed amount of £5 and offer a prize draw

31.3.79 DWIA Annual General Meeting (AGM) at Pear Tree House (60 members in attendance)

As part of the chairman report he informed members present of proposed plans for next year (1980). As part of generating funds for DWIA building a possible shareholders co-op in which members would contribute £5 per year and an annual prize draw to be included

22.4.79 DWIA Management committee meeting at The Havana Night Club

Urban Aid update – Derbyshire County Council (DerbyShire CC) letter outlined the procedures on the purchase of property for a community / cultural centre. Members accepted the suggested procedure and Derbyshire County Council to act as the agent for DWIA in the purchasing of any property for the community / cultural centre. Derby City Council letter received stating there was no available land at present and the matter would be discussed at the next council meeting for Rose Hill / Pear Tree district plan working group.

10.5.79 DWIA Management committee meeting at The Havana Night Club

Urban Aid update- Secretary stated St Augustine Church Hall was now up for sale and Derbyshire County Council asked to negotiate on DWIA's behalf for the purchase of the hall.

24.6.79 DWIA Special Management committee meeting at The Havana Night Club

Urban Aid – Purchasing Process: Members expressed their concerns regarding Derby City Council (DCC) processes that were adopted in the negotiations used for the purchasing of St Augustine's Church Hall. Members felt DCC had excluded DWIA which created difficulties for DWIA and timescale for this process was very long. Members agreed to meet with DCC leader (Mr Walker) to obtain more facts about the process adopted by DCC, and write to the church expressing concerns regarding the unfair treatment. If the meeting with DCC leader has not provided any satisfactory answers to questions raised then the matter would be taken further with possible option to write to MP's.

30.6.79 DWIA membership meeting at Pear Tree House, 30 members in attendance

Urban Aid update - Derby City Council had purchased St Augustine's Church Hall for their own use and the sub-committee and full committee were disappointed with the process. A meeting with DCC will be arranged seeking more support to aid DWIA secure a building. A letter will be sent to Derbyshire County Council seeking clarification how long the loan can be kept for until it was spent

Derbyshire County Council letter – expressing doubt that the urban aid grant being held over for another year after March 1980. (5) Reverend Osbourne replied to DWIA letter

Children and young people visiting the newly-built centre

stating the church hall has a covenant against license premises and the church decision was not based on any racial bias or basis

22.7.79 DWIA Management committee meeting at The Havana Night Club

The Secretary informed members that he wrote to the Leader of Derby City Council (Cllr Mick Walker) who responded by a telephone call and confirming a meeting would be arranged however no date was set during the telephone conversation. Members agreed to a follow up letter to DCC Leader

Members agreed that an "all out" effort to be made to find a suitable building for DWIA. The Apollo Shop was considered and enquiries should be made

28.8.79 DWIA Management committee meeting at The Havana Night Club

Urban Aid update - The Secretary informed members that an official application was submitted to Derbyshire County Council for a

lease of part of the Castle School on Traffic Street. DWIA was now awaiting a reply from the County Council.

The meeting with Derby City Council Leader Cllr Mick Walker concluded with a promise from Cllr Walker of a piece of land in the castle ward for a new build at a cost of £2,000 rent per year. Members discussed at great length and agreed to go for an existing building as option one and if all building options are exhausted then the least preferred option would be used to purchase land for a new build

6.10.79 DWIA membership meeting at Pear Tree House (45 members in attendance)

Question from the membership: What was the position on the Urban Aid?
Answer: The Secretary responded by reading a letter from Derbyshire County Council that gave a detailed update which included the difficulties Derbyshire County Council could have if the grant allocated to DWIA was not

spent and required another further extension, and it would be better to spend the grant by March 1980.

Urban Aid update - The Chairman gave a summary overview for the members:

- 6 properties have been looked at since the grant was received and all had building problems which made them unsuitable especially when considering the long-term use.
- The grant was frozen until December
- The application submitted to Derbyshire County Council for Castle School was in competition with Royal Mail who were favourites to obtain the building
- If no suitable building could be found as a last resort a piece of land would be purchased with the yearly rental of £2,000 ensuring a new build for DWIA community/culture centre. To date no reply had been received from Derbyshire County Council regarding the sale of the Castle School which was considered not to be a good sign.
- The Secretary read a letter sent to the Director of Education and Derbyshire County Council Chairman Mr Norman Wilson requesting their support to purchase Castle School.
- Regarding the land option it was agreed that the DWIA committee and sub-committee will be undertaking further work to look at all the key points for and against the land option.

At this meeting DWIA received a petition signed by 99 young people demanding DWIA find them a place soon was considered to be difficult to accept given all the work committee members had already undertaken to secure the purchase of a building. The Chairman suggested a meeting with the young people would be a positive way forward to discuss their concerns.

7.10.79 DWIA Special Management committee meeting at The Havana Night Club

The meeting was called to discuss a document from Derby City Council for leasing a piece of land to build a centre for DWIA with the annual rental cost of £2,000. As this was the last resort members agreed to take further action to secure the Castle School and ask two local MP's for their support. In doing so the MP's should be invited to the next meeting.

The Chairman said as the £2,000 lease rental cost would be an annual payment it would need the approval of the membership

4.11.79 DWIA Special Management committee meeting at The Havana Night Club

Correspondences – Mr Walter Johnson wrote and confirmed he would meet with members of DWIA to discuss DWIA grant and any other concerns DWIA had. The Chairman confirmed that any committee member could attend.

2.12.79 DWIA Special Management committee meeting at The Havana Night Club

Correspondence - Mr Walter Johnson MP sent a copy of a letter he received from Derbyshire County Council regarding the Urban Aid. Mr Johnson would be writing to DWIA shortly after his meeting with the Derbyshire County Council Chairman

Urban Aid - There was no further report or update from Derbyshire County Council regarding the grant. Members agreed that an offer could be made for St James Church Hall as soon as we had further information and the position of the grant

2.1.80 DWIA Management committee meeting at Madeley Centre

Correspondences (1) Mrs Buchanan thanks DWIA for the wreath sent for Mr Buchanan's funeral. (2) Pennine Hotel confirms booking for the Independence Dinner and Dance. (3) Derby City Council seeking clarification from DWIA regarding the lease of the land and to inform them by 11th February 1980 if this option will be taken up or not. (4) Mr Walter Johnson MP sends a copy of a letter received from Derbyshire County Council Chairman. (4) Mr Phillip Whitehead also sends his letter that he received from The Chief Executive Officer Mr Ashcroft. (5) Jamaica Prime Minister sends a Christmas

Urban Aid - DWIA received a letter from Derbyshire County Council Chairman Mr Walter Johnson highlighting St James Church Hall was in need of repairs to bring the building up to the required building standards and the grant allocation was not enough to cover such repairs. It was also noted the building was not in full use. Members felt that DWIA could apply to Derby City Council for an additional grant to cover the repair costs. The Secretary's letter to Rolls Royce in search of a building to date had not been successful.

15.3.80 DWIA Management committee meeting at Madeley Centre

Correspondences (1) The Department of the Environment confirmed DWIA grant will run into 1981. (2) UKIAS invites two DWIA members to their annual conference to be held on 12-13 April. (3) Pennine Hotel confirms DWIA booking for the Easter dance. (4) Derbyshire County Council letter gives a report on 35-37 Hartington Street.

Urban Aid – The Secretary gave an up-to-date report of the grant. St James Church originally refused to sell but now have promised they will look again at DWIA offer

A house in Charnwood Street was for sale and was being looked at as an option. The committee agreed to investigate more and if possible try and buy it. The Chairman reminded the committee that there a sub committee consisting of DWIA Chairman, Secretary, and Treasurer who would investigate this and other options. As suggested by members which meant the sub-committee should look at the education building in Becket Street.

22.3.80 DWIA Membership meeting at Pear Tree House, 22 members in attendance

Correspondences - Derby City Council letter confirming DWIA is now registered to do lottery

Urban Aid

- The Secretary gave members an up-to-date report on the urban aid grant
- The grant would be extended up to 1981
- Awaiting a report from Derbyshire County Council on a building DWIA building sub-committee looked at in Charnwood Street
- DWIA's ambition to buy St James Church Hall was rejected at a Parish meeting, however the church promised to look again at DWIA's offer. A decision is expected from their church after Easter. The Chairman informed members that a lot of work had been undertaken by the sub-committee to search and find a building which was not recorded and it was important that members were aware of this as everyone wanted a successful end to the process which is to have a building that meets the needs of DWIA

Treasurer's report

Mr Lee informed members that DWIA fundraising was not as predicted and as such had an impact on other activities. The following detail highlighted the current balance of each DWIA bank account

- The building fund £958.18
- The Savings / investment £1 024.03
- The Current account £264.77

The Chairman and Mr Gordon thanked the Treasurer for spending time and effort to ensure DWIA's accounts were up-to-date.

3.5.80 DWIA Management committee meeting at Madeley Centre

Correspondences - The Reverend Arthur Spencer wrote to inform DWIA that his church could not offer any accommodation at Gordon Street Methodist Church

Urban Aid update
- Members were informed that DWIA lost the purchase of St James by one vote
- Mr Murray read out two draft letters to be sent to Derbyshire County Council and Sport Council. Members made two minor amendments and approved the letters be signed by all committee members
- Members were informed that The Carib Club was up for sale at £100,000. There was a discussion on how to raise the funds to buy property. It was agreed that Mr McBean, Mr Murray and Mr Lee would contact Derbyshire County Council to explore the possibilities of purchasing the Carib club.
- Mr McBean wrote off any enquiry about the sale of Pear Tree House to DWIA

21.6.80 DWIA Special Management committee meeting at The Havana Night Club

Correspondence
Derbyshire County Council wrote to inform members that Councillor Mr G.R. Thomas and

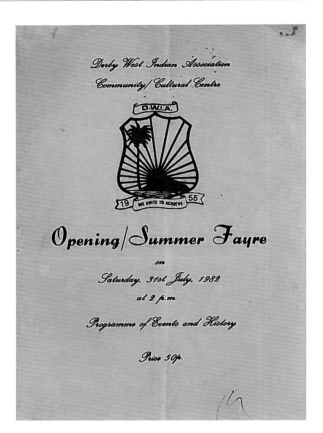

Opening of the first phase of the building by the High Commissioner of Trinidad and Tobago

Mr A. Wright have again been appointed to serve on DWIA management committee.

Sports Council replied to DWIA application for a sports grant and would be happy to meet on the site. Mr. Logan had met some members of the Committee and suggested the Association submit a full architect report of the buildings in Becket Street

26.6.80 DWIA membership meeting at Pear Tree House 35 attended

Correspondences
The Sport Council - suggesting DWIA should seek advice and guidance from a building surveyor before entering any negotiations for purchasing the building in Becket Street.

Urban Aid
The Secretary gave an up-to-date report on the situation regarding the search for a property. He

FOREWORD

The cancellation of our Carnival this year has been met with disappointment from many who look forward to what has become our Annual Festivity. However, the Committee felt that they could not possibly cope with all the work that is involved in putting on the Carnival, and the numerous commitments in getting the first phase of the Community/ Cultural Centre operational. To be fair, it seems as if it is always the faithful few who repeatedly carry the burden of the work, hence a priority had to be made.

Today, after all the years of struggle we have come to what must be considered a remarkable achievement for the West Indian people of Derby. The opening of this Centre is, I hope a turning point in our fortunes and the beginning of an era where unity and community spirit will take precedent over insularity.

I hope that ideas and activities will come from the wider community so as to make maximum use of the available space. At the moment there are a number of activities and clubs already operating at the Centre, but any group needing information regarding their own activities can contact the Youth/Community Worker, any other Committee Member or myself.

It is imperative that in this time of high unemployment, other social ills and lack of facilities, the community should remain united as a source of strength.

I do hope that the opening of this first phase of the project will inspire each and every West Indian in Derby to contribute in cash and kind, so that the remaining phase which comprises of a bar, library, a big hall and other amenities, can soon be built to provide the much needed social and educational meeting place for the large number of our unemployed youth.

I welcome you all and wish you a pleasant and enjoyable day at the "Fayre."

S. A. WALTERS
President.

TIME TABLE OF EVENTS

1.30 p.m.	The President of the Association welcomes and receives guests. A glass of sherry will be served to each guest.
1.45 p.m.	Steel Band
2.00 p.m.	The President calls the function to order. The President will give a brief speech.
	The Secretary of the Association will present a brief history of the Association on behalf of Mr. McBean (Ex-Secretary of the Association).
	The President will call upon the Mayor to give Civic greetings.
	The President will call upon the Lord Lieutenant to give a speech.
	The President will call upon the High Commissioner for Trinidad and Tobago - Eustace Seignoret to give a speech.
2.50 p.m.	The President will ask the Mayor and Lord Lieutenant to declare the Centre officially open.
3.00 p.m.	President thanks Official guests.
3.10 p.m.	Buffet for Official guests.
3.45 p.m.	Entertainment by the Steel Band - Hardwick Girl's Junior.
4.15 p.m.	The Musical Youth - a group from Birmingham.

FOOD STALLS

RICE AND CURRY	GAMES
GOAT	PRIZE DRAWS
CAKES	MUSIC

BRIEF HISTORY OF THE DERBY WEST INDIAN ASSOCIATION

The first seed of the Derby West Indian Association was sown in 1955 when a group of West Indians in Derby met in a house of a friend to discuss unity and survival in a foreign land. However, the Association proper was formed in December 1961, and the following is a quotation from the Minutes of that Meeting.

"A draft Constitution was presented to the audience, which numbered well over 100, for their approval, and after a few minor changes it was unanimously agreed that the draft Constitution be accepted. It was also agreed that the name of the organisation should be the 'Derby West Indian Association.' The election of Officers took place under the guidance of Mr. A. Bethume - Community Development Welfare Officer of the Migrant Services Department of the Jamaica High Commission." (Mr. Bethume has now been dead for some years).

"The following persons were elected as Officers for the period of one year.

Dr. C. E. Meade	-	President
Mr. Hill	-	Vice President
Mr. M. S. Douglas	-	Secretary
Mr. R. Barnes	-	Asst. Secretary
Mr. C. C. McBean	-	Treasurer."

Since that time several attempts have been made to establish a Centre but without success. In 1977 Mr. S. A. Walters became President and the search for some base for the West Indian Community again began in earnest. With the help and advice of the Derby Council for Voluntary Services, an application was made to the Department of the Environment for a grant towards what was called a "Day Centre", with a hall to provide accommodation for 200 people, a Nursery, a room for the elderly West Indians, a Library, Office, Committee Room, Indoor Games equipment and furnishing. However, the application failed. An application in 1977/78 for £4,000 was successful, at that time most people felt our problems were over.

A Steering Committee was quickly set up with representatives from the County Council, C.R.E. members of our Committee and members of the Community. A number of buildings were looked at including the Unity Hall, St. Augustine Church Hall and St. James's Church Hall, but they all fell through. Help was sought from all quarters, including Church bodies and M.P.'s, while the search for an appropriate building went on without much success and the threat of the grant being frozen and/or withdrawn. A reprieve of the grant with an extension of one year, to be taken up in 1980/81 delighted the Committee, who had not weakened in their resolve, inspite of repeated failures.

A final attempt was made to the City Council for help to find a site for the Centre. A meeting with Councillor Mick Walker and Mr. Cowlishaw, members of the Steering Committee and Mr. Crosdale - Community Relations Officer, proved to be successful in obtaining the plot of land on which the Centre now stands. This land was bought and paid for by the City Council at a cost of £9,000.

Through all these ups and downs there are a number of people who need special mention, they are :-

Mr. Charles White, Mr. Brian Ambrose, Mr. Scott, Mr. Humpston, Mr. Taylor, Mr. Calladine, Mr. Milton Crosdale, and Members of our Committee, without whose help we would never have reached where we are today.

confirmed there was nowhere suitable, and the search was becoming more difficult. Members were informed that DWIA was not getting any help from the County or Derby City Council.

Members suggested that a letter be sent to the Mayor requesting a meeting with the Council. The Chairman appealed to members for continual support of the Association and acknowledged those members who always give their time and support. A special mention was given to Mr. Murray, Mr. Lee and Mr. Mighty for their support to the organisation.

26.9.80 DWIA membership meeting at Pear Tree House 35 attended

Urban Aid - The Secretary reported on the latest development of the Urban Aid programme. He stated the Association will be interviewing candidates on the 11th August for the Youth and Community worker's post. In addition, reported a meeting with Councillor Mick Walker and Ray Cowlishaw proved successful, as the Association was looking at Cosmo Cinema, with an interest to buy the property.

13.9.80 DWIA Management committee meeting at Madeley Centre

Derbyshire County Council sent a full report on the Cosmo Cinema and the cost of the new building on the land. After discussion the Committee voted, 12 agreed to proceed with the land project and 2 abstained, it was agreed to pursue the land offer. The Chairman thanked Mr. Crosdale for his help with this matter.

11.10.80 DWIA Management committee meeting at Madeley Centre

Urban Aid

The Secretary gave members an up-to-date report, at the last meeting. Mr Calladin - Derbyshire County Council architects would be working on the project in order to get the necessary plans in place.

The new land identified was in the Castle industrial area.

13.12.80 DWIA Management committee meeting at Madeley Centre

Urban Aid Public meeting - Mr Lee gave a report on the first meeting of the fundraising committee which was launched at the public meeting (29th November). To date nine (9) people had donated £5 towards the centre, and he was looking at an incentive scheme for people to become collectors for the fundraising campaign

The fundraising campaign which saw DWIA membership grow along with fundraising activities such a raffles etc, £5 a brick concepts were used to drive campaign and capture the philanthropic actions from all supporters of DWIA establishing a community / cultural centre in Derby. A total of £2 800 was raised by 1981 (equivalent to £10,373.15 in 2022)

The minutes book does not reflect any further information regarding the actual building phase; however, it can be assumed that there was no major problem to hinder progress and any snags (repairs) associated with new build were dealt with under the builder's responsibility and for an agreed time

During 1981/82, the builders worked hard and maintained building regulations to ensure the building was fit for purpose. Regular checks were made by Derby City Council building officials and DWIA members to measure progress and/or raise any issues.

Journey Towards Sustainability

DWICA's Sustainability Plan to help the organisation survive and thrive involves the self-generation of funds through the rental of its building, car park and the development of its warm hub kitchen and social club as a commercial venture.

As a voluntary community association and a charity, DWICA also seeks funding and support from non-governmental bodies, trusts and foundations.

DWICA is grateful to the following organisations that have provided funding and support over many years to enable the Association to deliver the many services and provisions to its members and the community at large.

- Derbyshire County Council, particularly under the leadership of Councillor Bookbinder, provided Core Funding and the establishment of DWICA's community centre
- Derby City Council, under the leadership of Councillor Bob Laxton, helped to secure the land on which the community centre is built. The council also provided core funding as a Unitary Authority for a limited time.
- Manpower Services Commission
- Youth Training Scheme (YTS)
- The Connexions Service
- Derby Pride
- Derbyshire Community Foundation
- BBC Children in Need – Summer School and Exclusion Project

- The National Lottery in 1997 – 3 years Youth Programme Project
- Learning and Skills Council – Community Development Project
- Big Lottery Reaching Community Fund 2018/22 – Stronger Together Project
- People's Health Trust – Healthy Active Lives Project
- The National Lottery Reaching Community Fund – Even Stronger Together Project 2023/26
- National Lottery Heritage Fund, The Centre that Powers the Rosad project
- Arts Council England – funding for Carnival through the National Portfolio Organisation, EMCCAN

Honouring the DWIA Credit Union: A Story of Dedication

In 1978, some members of the Derby West Indian Association had difficulty saving and borrowing money for major purchases including overseas holidays. To address this issue, three dedicated members of the Association set out to explore the possibility of establishing a credit union. After their research into their legal obligations and what was required to meet the criteria of a common bond, the DWIA executive committee welcomed members to the DWIA Credit Union on 11 October 1980. Later that year, on 13 December, the Secretary, George Mighty, advised members that the DWIA Credit Union had been officially approved and was ready to lend money.

Throughout the years, the credit union flourished and, in 2005, was awarded a recognition award by the East Midlands Regional Chapter for 25 years of successful growth and development while providing a valued financial support service to the community. By the time it celebrated its 30th year, it boasted over 250 members.

In order to broaden its membership base and to provide a long-term option, the DWIA executive developed processes for non-members to join.

In 2011, the common bond was transferred to a new city-wide credit union called the Derby United Credit Union, at which point DWIA no longer had any legal duties or responsibilities for its operations.

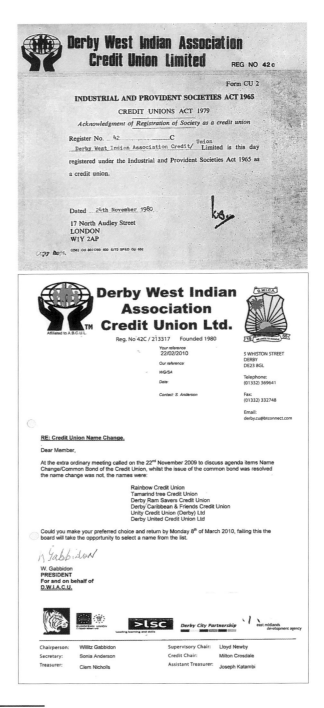

Derby West Indian Association Credit Union Ltd

Minutes of the Extra – ordinary meeting held on 22 November 2009 at the Derby West Indian Association Credit Union

Present

M. Crosdale
W. Gabbindon
C Nicholls
O. Marr (Mrs)
A. Crosdale
M. Pitter
D. Hamilton
Cecile Wright
Kalon Richards
Z. Blunt
N. Blunt
J. Katambi

Apology

S. Crosdale
Lucil Smith (Mrs)
Miss Taylor
Mrs Dimale
Mr Walford Francis
T. Crosdale

The meeting commenced at 16.10 and was quorate.

The chairman's overview

The Chairperson's overview provided information concerning the context and rationale for the extra ordinary members' meeting. This meeting dealt with one item only namely the proposed change to the Common Bond and to the name of the Credit Union. The discussion / overview dealt with the following issues:

- Financial sustainability
- Widening the membership e.g. extension of geographical base
- Scope / Opportunity for the Credit Union to reflect the relevant social public agenda i.e. financial social inclusion and to widen our membership. This would also enhance our financial sustainability.
- Renaming the credit union to make it more inclusive.

- Informed members of previous Board discussions on future strategic direction
- Informed members of cessation of operations of another existing credit union, which offered the opportunity to enhance our membership.

Common Bond

The discussion focussed on the widening of the membership and extension of the geographical area, accordingly. The changes also take account of matters relating to financial / social inclusion e.g. becoming Derby wide.

Resolved:

It was resolved that there should be:

- Widening of the membership
- Expansion of the geographical area.
- To respond as appropriate to relevant social agenda.

Name change

The name change needed to take account of the above aspects relating to the Common Bond. The following names were proposed:

- Derby Ram Savers
- Caribbean & Friends
- Tamarind Tree
- Rainbow Credit Union
- Any other preferred name

Resolved:

It was resolved to seek assistance from Derby University and Derby Homes with the marketing and possible logo. It was further resolved to canvass the membership regarding the chosen name.

The meeting closed at 16.55 hours.

The Benevolent Fund

Derby West Indian Association (DWIA) Members recognised that there was a need to set up a Sick Benefit Fund to provide financial support for those who did not qualify for government sick pay and to ease the stress of not having any income to provide for their family. This was called 'The Benevolent Fund' which was managed by DWIA elected executive management committee members. All related discussions would take place at executive management committee and / or at full members' meetings.

In March 1974, the Benevolent Fund was established at a DWIA members' meeting and subscription started at 10 pence per week (approximately £1.23 today).

The Benevolent Fund ran for six years until 13 December 1980. At this stage, DWIA members were working taxpayers and as such became eligible for 'Invalidity Benefit', the UK's National Insurance scheme introduced in 1971 for employees who had been invalided out of their trade or occupation after sustaining an injury. This is known today as Statutory Sick Pay (SSP).

At a DWIA members' meeting on Saturday 13 December 1980, held at the Madeley Centre in Madeley Street, Derby, the membership accepted the executive management committee proposal that the remaining balance of the Benevolent Fund, in the amount of £853.86 (approximately £3,900 today) should be used to pay out during the Christmas festive season.

The table below is a summary of the timeline and development process of the Fund over the life of the project (all funds have been recalculated to show current day value in 2023)

Date	Venue	Information from the original DWIA Executive Management Meeting Minutes' Books
16.3.74	Pear Tree House	**Members' Meeting** – Attendance: 45 The President in his opening address made the following suggestions; the setting up of a Benevolent Scheme which members could contribute to and receive benefits when sick.
01.6.74	Pear Tree House	**Members' Meeting** – 45 members in attendance (over 350 paid up registered members) Clarification regarding the Benevolent Club, The president informed members that all systems were now in place to start collecting membership subscriptions of 10 pence per week and fund collectors are Mr Mitchell, Mr Walter, Mrs V O Connor and Mr V Martin. Other collectors to be recruited at a later stage.

26.10.74 Pear Tree House **Members' Meeting** – 35 members attended

Members asked for an update on the Benevolent Fund to which the Chairman informed members that 103 members registered and to date £26 (*£288.73*)

8.3.75. Pear Tree House **AGM**

Election Results

President: Mr SA Walter; Vice President: Mr H Phillips; Secretary: Mr C C McBean; Assistant Secretary: Mrs A M Ashby; Treasurer: Mr J Gordon; Assistant Treasurer: Mr R S Reid; Committee Members: Mr & Mrs O Connor, Mr G Davidson, Mr H Emmanuel, Mr Mitchell, Mr J Scott, Miss P Clarke Miss N V Hudson, Mr M Reid, Mr C Hill, Mr W Gabbidon, Mrs K Ashby, Mr R G Newman, Mrs V Martin

Benevolent Fund established and had £448.79 (*£4 011.39*) in the fund and 80 members. DWIA Benevolent Fund – Mrs O Connor and Mrs. Martin were elected as Treasurer and Assistant Treasurer respectively.

26.4.75 Pear Tree House **Members' Meeting** – 65 members in attendance

Benevolent Fund members agree to have an update meeting.

05.07.75 Pear Tree House **Members' Meeting** – 40 members attended

Benevolent Fund (Sick benefit fund) update - £555.46 (*£4 964.83*) in a separate account at the Nat West Bank

11.2.76 25 Crewe Street **Executive Meeting**

£10 (*£76.69*) to be donated to a member from the Benevolent Fund as a result of long-term illness.

6.3.76 Pear Tree House **DWIA AGM** – 67 members attended

Chairman's Report – £279 (*£2 139.78*) was paid out to members from the Benevolent Fund which was set up for people who did not receive any sick benefit from the government. The Benevolent Fund Treasurer (Mrs V O'Connor) reported the fund was in a healthy position

Election of Officers – Mr R S Walters, President (Chairman); Mrs N V O 'Connor, Vice President; Mr C C McBean, Secretary; Mrs A M Ashby, Assistant Secretary; Mr J Gordon, Treasurer; Mr R S Reid, Assistant Treasurer

DWIA members – Mr S Mitchell, Mr G Davidson, Mr H Emmanuel, Mr J Harewood, Mr Frazer, Mr G Williamson, Mr S Lee, Mr O'Connor, Mrs Douce, Miss N V Hudson, Mrs E Francis (Benevolent Fund assistant secretary) Mr J Scott, Mr K Ashby

Co-opted members – Mr H Francis, Mr L Bennett, Mr J Smith (presiding officer over the election process)

15.5.76 Pear Tree House DWIA Chairman congratulates Mrs Francis (DWIA Benevolent Fund Assistant Treasurer) on her new appointment to Derby Police Constabulary as a special constable (WPO)

23.10.76 Pear Tree House Benevolent Fund Proposal – cash back scheme £5 (£38.35) at the end of the 1st year and £10 (*£76.69*) in the 2nd year and £5 in the 3rd year.

This proposal would be put to DWIA full membership at the next membership meeting

27.11.76 Pear Tree House **Members' Meeting**

Benevolent Fund cash back scheme approved as £5 in year 1 £10 in year 2 and £5 in year 3

23.4.77 Pear Tree House **AGM**

Benevolent Fund report £732.72 *(£5 619.58)* in the fund and no sick benefit was claimed – report accepted by membership

Chairman's Report – Gave positive encouragement with regard to the Benevolent Fund and encourage those members who had not joined the fund to do so.

Election of officers (Mr M S Douglas presided over the election process): President (chairman), Mr S A Walters; Vice President, Mr J Gordon; Secretary, Mr C C McBean; Assistant Secretary, Miss N V Hudson; Treasurer, Mr S Lee; Assistant Treasurer, Mrs E Francis

Committee members: Mrs A M Ashby, Mr G Mighty, Mr G Williamson, Mr G Davidson, Mr L Bennett, Mrs N O'Connor, Mr S Mitchell, Mr R Fraser, Mrs L Blunt, Mrs Williamson, Mr B Williams, Mr A Hutchinson

11.2.78 Pear Tree House **Executive Management Meeting**

Treasurer's financial report – DWIA Benevolent Fund *(£4 032.94)*

13.8.78 The Havana Club The Chairman then announced the death of member who had contributed to the Benevolent Fund, members agreed to make an additional donation from the fund to go supporting the family to meet the funeral costs.

The Treasurer also suggested DWIA should look at a possible insurance for the Benevolent Fund

31.3.79 Pear Tree house **AGM** – 60 members in attendance

Treasurer's report (Mr S Lee) – explained to members that the proposed changes to DWIA constitution would improve the management and performance of the organisation. In addition, a new format for presenting the accounts was used to inform members in detail of the financial position of the organisation, this included the introduction of an organisational financial balance sheet. The Treasurer confirmed the following: - DWIA General account: £502.51, Trustee Saving Bank (TSB) £1 024. Festival account £577.92, Benevolent Fund £842 (today's value *£4 539)*

Election of Officers which was conducted by Mr M S Douglas

President: Mr S Walters, Vice President: Mr J Gordon Secretary: Mr CC McBean Assistant Secretary Miss NV Hudson Treasurer: Mr S Lee Assistant Treasurer: Mrs E Francis

Executive committee: Mr G Davidson Mr J Smith, Mrs P Gabbidon, Mrs M Williamson, Mr L Bennet, Mr G Mighty, Mr R Fraser, Mrs A M Ashby Mr D Williamson, Mrs N Wright, Mr T Brown and Mrs L Blunt.

6.10.79 Pear Tree House **Members' Meeting** – 45 members in attendance

Benevolent Fund. The Chairman raised concerns that the scheme had become dormant and a meeting of Benevolent Fund members would be called to discuss the best way forward.

Members agreed to send Mr Douglas, Mr Williamson and Mr Patterson some fruits

3.5.80 Madeley Centre **Executive Management Meeting**

Members agreed to honour a request for financial funds and will be paid from the Benevolent Fund

28.6.80 Pear Tree House **Members' Meeting** – 35 members

Benevolent Fund: The Chairman confirmed the fund had now closed and all members had received the funds they have paid in. Furthermore, would welcome those members who wish to donate their funds paid into the Benevolent Fund to the Association and would contact all members concerned.

11.10.80 Madeley Centre **Executive Management Meeting**

The Benevolent Fund has £968.72 *(£4 426.19)*. This will be paid out to members at the end of the meeting.

13.12.80 Madeley Centre **Executive Management Meeting**

Benevolent Fund – A balance of £853 .86 *(£3 901.38)* was recorded and arrangements were being made to pay out to members for Christmas.

DWICA Burial Plot

In addition to the Benevolent Fund, one of the aims of our pioneers in establishing a Community Association (DWICA) was to look at unity and survival in a foreign land. 'Safety in numbers' was one of their main objectives.

These early Pioneers were both sympathetic and caring in terms of taking care of individuals in the community. As proud members of the West Indian community they had also determined that no member of our community would end up in a 'pauper's grave'.

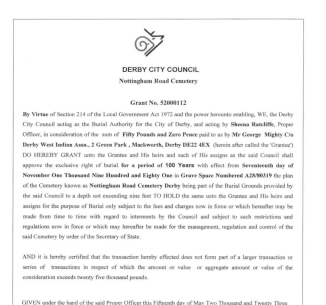

DERBY CITY COUNCIL
Nottingham Road Cemetery

Grant No. 52000112

By Virtue of Section 214 of the Local Government Act 1972 and the power hereunto enabling, WE, the Derby City Council acting as the Burial Authority for the City of Derby, and acting by **Sheena Ratcliffe**, Proper Officer, in consideration of the sum of **Fifty Pounds and Zero Pence** paid to us by **Mr George Mighty C/o Derby West Indian Assn., 2 Green Park , Mackworth, Derby DE22 4EX** (herein after called the 'Grantee') DO HEREBY GRANT unto the Grantee and His heirs and such of His assigns as the said Council shall approve the exclusive right of burial **for a period of 100 Years** with effect from **Seventeenth day of November One Thousand Nine Hundred and Eighty One** in Grave Space Numbered **A28/80319** the plan of the Cemetery known as **Nottingham Road Cemetery Derby** being part of the Burial Grounds provided by the said Council to a depth not exceeding nine feet TO HOLD the same unto the Grantee and His heirs and assigns for the purpose of Burial only subject to the fees and charges now in force or which hereafter may be made from time to time with regard to interments by the Council and subject to such restrictions and regulations now in force or which may hereafter be made for the management, regulation and control of the said Cemetery by order of the Secretary of State.

AND it is hereby certified that the transaction hereby effected does not form part of a larger transaction or series of transactions in respect of which the amount or value or aggregate amount or value of the consideration exceeds twenty five thousand pounds.

GIVEN under the hand of the said Proper Officer this Fifteenth day of May Two Thousand and Twenty Three

Signed by the said Sheena Ratcliffe ....

In the presence of ....

The Deed to the Burial Plot

In November 1981, a member of our community died with no means to bury her, and with no family. DWICA was called upon to ensure that she was not buried in a pauper's grave. The Association, although having no permanent base or premises at the time, found the cash to purchase a burial plot for the interment of three individuals. The last interment took place in 1992.

DWICA's present management committee has proposed to erect a headstone bearing the names, ages and dates of interment the people buried in the grave.

The History of the Saturday School

In April 1975 at a DWIA members meeting, held at Pear Tree House, with 65 in attendance, four local schoolteachers gave a presentation, sharing with parents and DWIA members positive feedback on their children's educational progress. The meeting welcomed the support from DWIA to lobby for the full quota of teachers per school. DWIA executive committee started to develop plans to establish a Saturday Morning Club for young people to be held at Pear Tree House.

In February 1976, DWIA executive agreed to set up a sub-committee to look at educational and cultural projects. By 1978, the Saturday school was formed by Mr F Best, Mr David Lake, Mr G Mighty, Mr Bennett, Mr Harewood Mr P Miller and Ms J Underwood in partnership with Pear Tree Community Centre and Counselling Advisory Service (CAS). The aim was to improve children's reading, mathematics, English and writing. Classes were free of charge and ran for two hours 10.00am – 12.00 midday.

In June 1978, DWIA donated £25 (£166 today 2022) towards a weekend conference for young people at Lea Green, Matlock in early July.

In November 1980, Mr R Murray, the Saturday School's Project Manager (and DWIA newsletter editor) explained to the DWIA management committee that the project needed evaluation, as he had concerns regarding staffing and attendance levels. As a result of a detailed project review discussion, it was agreed that changes needed to be made to ensure a good quality service was delivered. In short, a Saturday school review restructure and rebranding process. DWIA agreed to develop the Saturday School underpinning it with a stable structure, an organised rota of volunteers and teachers who would oversee a return to good attendance.

With the new community / cultural centre in Carrington Street, DWICA management committee could plan with assurance knowing the location was not subject to any difficulties (e.g. external bookings, etc.). DWICA Saturday school developed during the 1980s, and in 1989 DWICA installed computers to improve organisational administration and projects such as the Saturday school. The active use of computers in the learning process was now a much-needed service at the Saturday School, with emphasis to active social and cultural learning activities.

DWICA, through feedback from parents / guardians and its members, recognised the high numbers of African Caribbean school students experiencing school exclusions for reasons which gave cause for concern. As such DWICA would, on request, attend with parents / guardians at school meetings to discuss their child's school exclusion.

1997 Saturday school – Development worker undertook actions to revive the Saturday school which includes recruiting volunteers for hands on duties to volunteers sitting on the Saturday school management board.

2005 Saturday school focuses on during 11am – 1.00pm - 5-16 year-old cohort by providing additional tuition in core curriculum subjects (Maths, Science, English) in addition to taking part in social learning activities within a cultural framework. To support the cohort development assessment are undertaken and compared to academic progress on a regular basis.

From 2010 until 2019, DWICA Saturday school project became dormant and as such the organisation had different projects young people were attending e.g. Summer School, Carnival troupe rehearsal. Both had active social skills learning underpinning all the activities.

In February 2020, DWICA volunteers rebranded the Saturday School programme to focus on personal development and targeted young people aged 8-15 years. Activities were designed to improve awareness of the young people's history/heritage and culture, whilst improving transferable skills (confidence, self-esteem, decision making, communication and problem solving). The Saturday school was going through a pilot scheme then the coronavirus pandemic in 2020 shut down the country. As a result of the pandemic, the explosion of social media, the organisation made use of its digital resources, to enable active social learning with this young people cohort during 2020-2022.

DWICA will continue to review its work with young people and establish a service created by young people for young people that promotes positive personal development, e.g. The Annual youth conferences is an event promoting positive opportunities for young people.

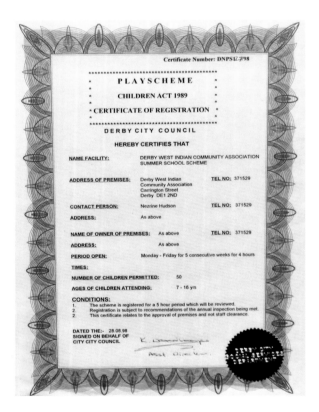

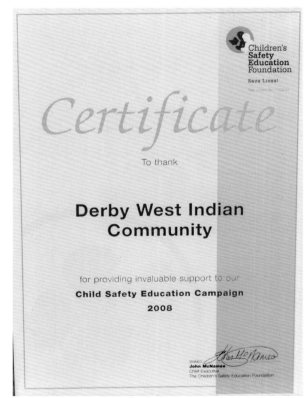

Parent Group

As a result of concerns raised by DWICA management and the community regarding young African Caribbean students in the school environment it became necessary to address this by forming a working group. Members of the community were invited to a meeting to create a parent forum on Saturday 24th March 2007 to discuss and agree various strategic approaches to address what was clearly an issue in the schools as the African Caribbean students were experiencing high levels of school exclusions.

The launch meeting was considered a success and it was attended by 33 people, with the guest speaker Patrick Augustus (author of *Baby Father* and *Weekend Father*) followed by questions & answers session.

DWICA management recognised this was not a new issue for the organisation, as in the 1970's they supported parents, students & schools to improve the school experience for all. DWICA had qualified and experienced people serving on the management board with particular skills and experience in the education institution processes and procedures. DWICA quickly got involved in addressing the concerns of parents in relation to their children's experience in the school settings.

The aim

- To improve the personal, social, and educational development of African

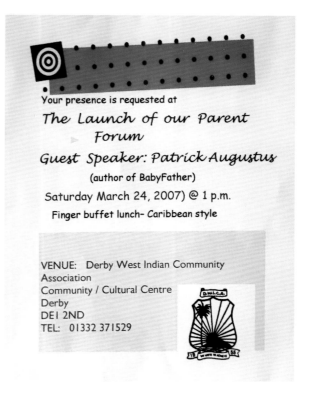

Your presence is requested at

The Launch of our Parent Forum

Guest Speaker: Patrick Augustus

(author of BabyFather)

Saturday March 24, 2007) @ 1 p.m.

Finger buffet lunch– Caribbean style

VENUE: Derby West Indian Community Association
Community / Cultural Centre
Derby
DE1 2ND
TEL: 01332 371529

Caribbean children through such development of their parents.
- To encourage parental involvement in the education of their children.

Key Objectives

- Disseminate information about admissions, exclusions procedures and other relevant issues.
- Provide one to one drop in for parents that require support.

- Representations on behalf of parents and pupils e.g. school Appeals meetings and parents evening.
- To signpost members to relevant services for young people in the city.

Derby Black Parents Forum

This forum had a constitution to manage the activities of the project whilst operating in a set of agreed rules to enable strategic development and involvement in matters of concern for parents/ guardians, students, and schools.

Some Key objectives of the forum were:

- To consult & engage with schools in the development of the curriculum.
- Promote partnership between parents/ guardians, pupils, and schools.

- To develop and engage in activities which support the education and welfare of the pupils.
- To represent parents at school meetings.
- Views on the education provided by the school and matters affecting the education and welfare of the students.

The forum had 29 registered members with regular attendance at monthly meetings of between eight and twelve parents/ guardians and DWICA members. It should be noted that the forum was managed by several DWICA volunteers, which included Maurice Lawrence (Chairman), Maureen Mosley (Secretary) and Annet Johnson (DWICA Education Assistant).

The History and Legacy of the DWICA Bursary Scheme

In August 1968, Derby West Indian Community Association members met at 25 Crewe Street and agreed to donate 25 guineas (about £370 today) to the 'Sir Alex Bustamante Foundation Scholarship', an organisation established by Jamaica's first Prime Minister to support the educational development of young people in Jamaica and other Caribbean islands.

At a DWIA meeting at Pear Tree House in August 1975, an educational bursary/scholarship scheme for 2nd and 3rd generation members of the Caribbean heritage community was discussed, with the executive meeting in January 1976 approving the scheme and considering increasing the membership fees to raise money for the awards.

April saw the implementation of a new application process and promotional drive, leading to five scholarships being awarded later that year to students attending college.

In 1996, DWICA donated £50 to Pear Tree Library in Normanton to mark the library's 80th year of service to the community.

Two years later, DWICA was congratulated by Community Matters (formerly the National Federation of Community Organisations) for introducing and maintaining the bursary scheme.

During the 2000s, five bursary awards were made to young people pursuing sports and two awards were made for higher education.

Currently, the educational bursary scheme is still providing support for the cost of course books and equipment, and DWICA has been offering vocational training courses for volunteers, such as those for the Summer School, Carnival costume design and make, marshal duties (LANTRA award), and Arts Award Assessor (Arts Council England), among others.

Initiative to Empower Young People

In 1985, the Derby West Indian Association led a community initiative to ensure African Caribbean young people in Derby had the opportunity to enrol on what was known as a 'Foundation Programme'. This initiative ensured 12 students of African Caribbean heritage received an income whilst studying up to A Level standard. This proved to be very popular amongst the African Caribbean community.

As a result of this successful 'Return to Learn' programme, and following interest from the Asian community, an additional 12 enrolment positions were added on to the course. In the first year, 24 students completed the course.

Some say it was the vision of the DWIA executive to address and improve community relations with the police and young people. Gaining the support of Derbyshire County Council was also a key factor towards the ultimate success of the programme.

The foundation course later became a mainstream access course open to those who wished to return to education.

DWICA Education Exclusion Project

As part of the organisation's commitment and drive for the academic and social development of young African Caribbean people in Derby, it was of concern that the organisation was receiving feedback from the community regarding school exclusions, and more concerning to note that whilst the overall rate of school exclusion had risen, it was significantly high in the African Caribbean community.

In September 2004, in partnership with BBC Children In Need Appeal, it set up the DWICA Exclusion Project. This much needed project was active until August 2008 and during this time directly supported 85 African Caribbean school students who were excluded or at risk of exclusion. A number of young people also benefited from informal support but which was not formally documented.

The aim of the project was to improve the academic performance of African Caribbean school pupils by raising the self-esteem and confidence of African Caribbean pupils in schools; helping to promote effective dialogue / networking between home and school / youth organisations; and promoting a positive attitude towards school and learning.

Services to help achieve these aims took place either at the school or at DWICA. These services included, one to one support and confidential advice; weekly Saturday schools; liaising regularly with school personnel, parents and other community-based organisations; and collating data from Derby City Council on African Caribbean school pupils.

The project was successful based on:

- The time spent on the planning stages and establishing useful contacts and networks that aided the delivery of the project.
- Schools recognised the benefit of the project and as such other organisations in the community were contacted e.g. Step Forward Educational Trust, the Pupil Referral Unit, Social Services, and the Department of Education and Skills
- Parents were made more aware of the school elusion project making them more aware of the issues relating to the education of their child(ren)
- The communication with parents improved and strengthened, especially on a one-to-one basis, and follow-up personal visits to the centre (as well as telephone calls) relating to their concerns about the school exclusion process.
- The positive outcomes from the young people that engaged in the project.

The History of Derby Caribbean Carnival

The Derby Caribbean Carnival is an annual arts, culture and recreational project/event planned and organised by the Derby West Indian Community Association (DWICA) for over forty-five years. Over the years it has grown from a local event to one with national recognition and covered by independent media companies and social platforms in the Caribbean and Africa, as well as viewed by audiences in the UK and Europe.

Derby Caribbean Carnival is by far the biggest and one of the longest-running projects the Association has managed.

The coronavirus pandemic resulted in a national lockdown of outdoor events and in Derby's case for two years (2020 & 2021). But it presented the opportunity for social media platforms to host virtual events. For DWICA it became clear that broadcasting Derby's Caribbean Virtual Carnival was the best option to meet popular demand and present an event that could be viewed by thousands without putting anyone at risk. The first year's broadcast was considered a success which led to even greater success the following year by having a live virtual performance by Beenie Man, an A-list dancehall artist from Jamaica. The event was watched by thousands across the globe.

It all started at DWIA's AGM in March 1975 when Mr Solomon 'Ricky' Walters was elected

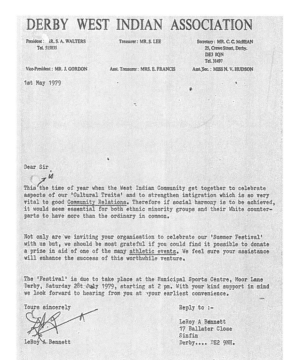

DWIA President and the creation of his flagship project to build a cultural legacy in Derby through artistic expression in a showcase manner by planning what was then known as the Derby Festival.

This was based on the success of DWIA's involvement in 1971 in the Derby Harmony Festival, and in the August 1974 participation in Derby Council for Community Relations festivals. In September 1974, the Council for Community Relations wrote a letter thanking DWIA for participating in the festival.

After tireless fundraising and planning, DWICA held their first 'Festival' of Caribbean Culture at Moorways sports stadium.

Sponsorship from local companies was sought in 1979. It is interesting to note that the companies were major employers in Derby and also employed many people from the Windrush generation.

The festival grew and in doing so was recognised as a project that could become a flagship for celebrating African Caribbean culture through creative arts. The event was later rebranded as the Derby Caribbean Carnival and by the late 1980s had embarked on organising the annual event that was attended by thousands.

DWICA then created a carnival promotion sub-group which toured many of the major carnivals in England (Birmingham, Leeds, Huddersfield, Preston, Leicester, Nottingham, Sheffield) to promote Derby Caribbean Carnival.

The events would also include live performances from artist such as Frankie Paul, Third World, Luciano, Wayne Wonder and Black Uhuru, to name just a few, as well as featuring major dancehall events by the UK's best sound systems, such as Saxon Studio, from London, Luv Injection, from Birmingham, Big Life Sound USA, from New Jersey, and World Class and World Sound Clash Champions, Bass Odyssey, from Jamaica.

Derby Caribbean Carnival now involves a Caribbean carnival procession with DWICA troupes, along with additional out of town troupes all representing various themes through their elaborate and spectacular costumes and dance routines.

The Carnival is now recognised by Derby City and Derbyshire County Council as the city's flagship event. It attracts thousands of visitors over the Carnival weekend and provides a welcome boost to the local economy.

As part of the continual growth of the Carnival it has engaged in partnerships with Derby

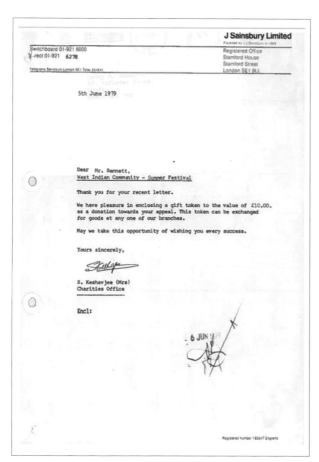

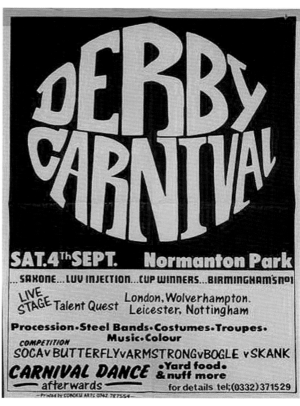

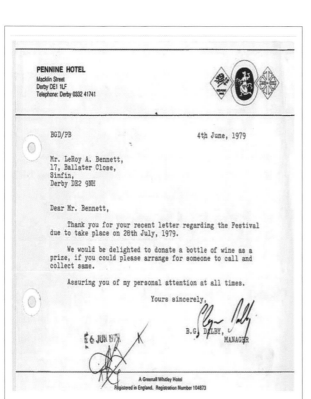

University, Derby Colleges, and various junior and secondary schools as part of the cultural and creative arts.

DWICA's Carnival volunteers have worked with leading carnival costume designers in the UK and the Bahamas and have gained many creative skills and techniques.

The carnival planning group at the time was led by Takyiwa Sankofa who recognised the importance of maintaining the cultural integrity of African Caribbean carnivals. The ethos included reflecting a more traditional Caribbean Carnival queen show; focussing on the costume design; involving steel bands and traditional carnival costumes; returning the carnival procession to the streets and including a large stage show; showcasing local talents and sound systems; attracting private sector sponsors and prizes; and bringing in international artists as well as those from across the UK. These aspects, and many others, enabled the Derby Caribbean Carnival to evolve from a marginal community event into the spectacular annual occasion we see today.

From street processions and live music performances, to food stalls, fairground rides and family fun-days, the Derby Caribbean Carnival is a feast for the senses.

DWICA Carnival troupe

Another area of growth over the years has been the DWICA Carnival troupes. With additional DWICA young people provision e.g. youth club, Saturday and summer school activities the development of DWICA troupes could be seen as a natural process.

With the expansion of additional carnival troupes across Derby, and the natural growth of DWICA carnival troupe the Branding and renaming of its carnival troupe from Derby Carnival Troupe to Cultural Roots Carnival Troupe (CRCT) in 2016 to provide its own sense of identity and open up opportunities for growth and development.

In April 2017, with the support of EMCCAN and Arts Council England, CRCT received funding which enabled it to produce the longest carnival touring programme they had done to

Miss Carnival Queen 1993

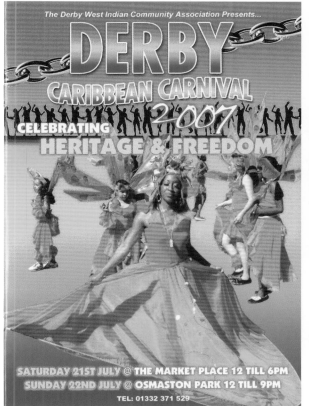

Derby Caribbean Carnival 2008

date. The tour included visits to Manchester, Luton, Leeds, Northampton, Nottingham, Birmingham, Leicester, Ashbourne, Long Eaton and the Isle of Wight.

With this newly established tour schedule, the drive for additional troupe members began with the aim of ensuring that there was full representation at each of these events. The opportunity to work with international choreographers such as ACE Dance & Music was an attractive opportunity for young people throughout Derby, as well as working with costume design and makers, Laura Hill and Jessica Kemp.

Having a larger team allowed the troupe to begin to enter more and more competitions. The year 2018 marked the first year that the troupe was able to enter a King, Queen, Prince and Princess into both the EMCCAN and Leeds competitions.

Additional activities include fundraising for these events; workshops for young people;

participation in carnival dance workshops with troupes in the Bahamas; and study visits to the Bahamas and Brazil to gain detailed knowledge and skills and techniques for carnival costume design and making.

Members of the CRCT back-office team is also acknowledged as the essential support team for all the troupes, enabling them to perform at their best. Recognition is also given to all the troupe parents who volunteer their time to the support the team especially during the busy CRCT carnival tour season. For the strategic and critical involvement in the creation and development of CRCT, a special vote of thanks goes to Tamara Rashford; Samantha Hudson; Niaz Stephenson; Maria Slack; Angella Mighty; Nezrine Hudson; and Mable Slater.

Derby Caribbean Carnival is still managed by DWICA which has a subgroup called Derby Caribbean Carnival Planning Group which has an open door approach to all positive

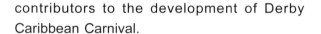

Derby Caribbean Carnival 2010

contributors to the development of Derby Caribbean Carnival.

Feeding the masses

Carnival catering has become a major operation to feed all troupes totalling in excess of four hundred members plus the marshals and other volunteers on events days. DWICA is forever grateful to the catering team for organising the planning, purchasing, cooking and distribution of meals on these occasions.

DWICA wishes to acknowledge the contributions of key people that have been part of the carnival growth and development journey. While it is not possible to include the names of all the volunteers, the Association acknowledges the following for their outstanding commitment to the DWICA carnival: Ses McDonald of Lonsdale Travel for sponsoring airline tickets to Jamaica for the Carnival Queen winner; Cleveland Chin for infrastructure logistics; Sam Lee for financial management

and logistics; Mr C. McBean for infrastructure logistics; Takyiwa Sankofa, Carnival project co-ordinator; May Bryant, Carnival chief chef and the other catering team members.

DCCPG meets on a regular basis all year round to plan the forthcoming carnival. The key principle behind the planning process is to encourage growth and development of African Caribbean cultural heritage / legacy through creative artistic expression.

DWICA is a key member of a regional partnership known as East Midlands Caribbean Carnival Arts Network (EMCCAN) a National Portfolio Organisation (NPO) recognised by Arts Council England. This partnership has representatives from Northampton, Leicester, Nottingham and Derby. It is well documented that Derby has been the lead member and continues to be a key member of the partnership and adheres to best management practices in the planning and delivery of Caribbean carnivals in the region and nationally.

Derby Caribbean Carnival 2010

Derby Caribbean Carnival 2011

Aswad performing at Derby Caribbean Carnival in 2011

Derby Caribbean Carnival 2011

Derby Caribbean Carnival 2011

Derby Caribbean Carnival 2012

Derby Caribbean Carnival 2012

Derby Caribbean Carnival 2012

Derby Caribbean Carnival 2014

Derby Caribbean Carnival 2014

Artistes performing at Derby Caribbean Carnival in 2014

Derby Caribbean Carnival 2014

Yashema McLeod performing at Derby Caribbean Carnival in 2015

Carnival preparations, 2015

Carnival preparations, 2015

Derby Caribbean Carnival 2015

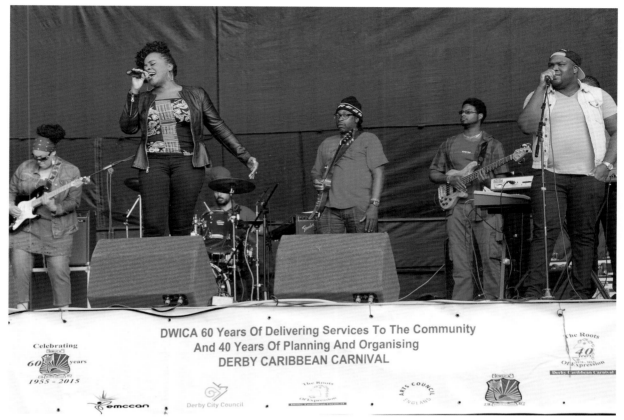

ETANA performing at Derby Caribbean Carnival in 2015

Sound system at Derby Caribbean Carnival in 2015

Derby Caribbean Carnival 2015

Derby Caribbean Carnival 2016

Derby Caribbean Carnival 2016

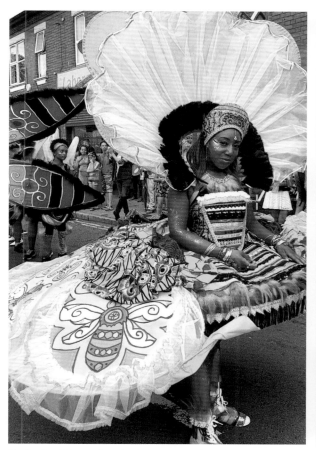

Derby Caribbean Carnival Queen, 2017

Derby Caribbean Carnival King, 2019

DWICA Soca Star Carnival trophy

Derby Caribbean Carnival 2022

Derby Caribbean Carnival 2022

Derby Caribbean Carnival 2022

Derby Caribbean Carnival 2022

Caribbean carnival celebrations in the UK

Caribbean carnival celebrations have been taking place in the UK since the 1950s, when large numbers of migrants from the Caribbean began to make the UK their home. These vibrant festivals of colour, music and dance have become deeply integrated into British culture, with cities across the nation hosting their own carnivals every year.

The most famous of these is Notting Hill Carnival, which is now Europe's largest street festival. It was established in 1959 and was first held as an indoor 'Caribbean Carnival' in St Pancras Town Hall in London. Now held every August Bank Holiday, Notting Hill Carnival sees up to two million people take to the streets in a vibrant display of spectacular costumes, set to the sounds of traditional and contemporary music and dance.

Leeds West Indian Carnival is another significant event, and has been celebrated every August since 1967. The carnival has become the biggest event of the year in Leeds and the celebration of Caribbean culture and art has become a much-loved part of the annual social calendar, with youth groups and sound systems taking to the streets alongside steel bands and traditional mas bands.

In addition to Notting Hill and Leeds, there are a variety of Caribbean carnivals that take place in cities throughout the UK every year, including Derby, Birmingham, Manchester, Leicester, Nottingham and Northampton.

These events are a celebration of the vibrancy of the Caribbean community and its culture, and are a colourful reminder of the unique and diverse nature of British society. They are a testament to the rich heritage and culture of British Caribbean communities and bring people together in a multicultural feast for the senses.

Heritage and Legacy Carnival costume 2022. Photo by Chevy-Jordan Thompson (Ofilaye)

Derby Caribbean Carnival 2022 – Costume Design and Make

DWICA in partnership with Derby Museum Project: 'The Centre that Powers the Road'
Costume title: Heritage and Legacy
Designed by: Samantha Hudson, DWICA and Steven Hoyte of Rampage
Construction: Steven Hoyte and DWICA Carnival Team

DESCRIPTION OF THE COSTUME

The Heritage and Legacy Carnival Costume portrays the building of the West Indian community in Derby and the transmission of West Indian culture. The costume expresses the development and achievements of the people who came from the Caribbean to the UK from the 1940s to present day. It demonstrates how they built a social, family and community life to support unity and survival in a foreign land.

The West Indian community established a Community Centre to support their activities and as a place to congregate and share common purposes. It also serves as a facility for other communities.

The Carnival costume depicts the DWICA logo and illustrates the Association's various activities such as cricket, darts and dominoes. The colours of orange, gold/yellow and blue represent the strength, spontaneity and cheerfulness of the West Indian people; the feathers represent strength, hope, freedom and spirit. *"We celebrate our freedom."*

DWIA Steel Band Project

The Pioneer Windrush generation grew up hearing Steel bands in the Caribbean, so it was no surprise that DWIA booked a steel band for its Jamaican Independence Dinner and Dance on 7th August 1964. Over the forthcoming years DWIA booked a number of steel bands to play at various DWIA social events including All Stars Steel Orchestra (London).

DWIA then created a sub-committee spearheaded by committee member Mr George Mighty to develop DWIA steel band project. The primary aim was to raise funds to purchase a full steel pan set.

1976 September - DWIA received a letter from the Community Relations Council informing them the funding application was unsuccessful. DWIA carried on their fundraising campaign and contact was made with Charlie Williams, Britain's first well-known Black stand-up comedian (as seen on TV) who agreed to attend a coffee evening as part of the fundraising activities.

1978 February - A letter from East Midlands Arts Association (now known as Arts Council England -ACE) confirming DWIA funding application had progress passed stage one. The application was successful.

1979 January - At DWIA AGM committee member Mr Mighty reported to members that the steel band sub-committee had purchased the steel drums and sub-committee members were seeking to raise funds to employ a full-time teacher for the band.

Recognising the social values of community cohesion, DWICA steel band project sub-group continued its campaign to include as part of the educational music workshop in schools, as a

DWICA newsletter, August 1980, above, featuring a short report from George Mighty (DWIA management committee) highlights the development of the project

Young people playing in the steel band

method to maintain cultural identity, self-esteem, a sense of purpose which in turn command the respect from the host community.

Out of this subgroup a sponsoring subgroup was formed with the following in mind:

1984 July – The West Indies cricket team visited Derby to play Derbyshire Cricket Club over two days (21st & 22nd July). The West Indies team were the guest of honour at DWIA on Saturday 21st July charity dance. The Littleover steel band performed on the night.

1987 – Derby Carnival week was delivered that consisted of a range of activities during the week including a carnival exhibition and a steel band show on Wednesday 9th September.

1988 Steel band – the equipment is loaned out to increase interest

With the generational change saw a drop in volunteer players, however, the DWICA kept the project in mind with the view to re-establish a DWICA steel band.

EMCCAN Community Steel Band (EMPAN)

In 2018/19, working as a key partner with the East Midlands Caribbean Carnival Arts Network (EMCCAN) developed a pilot scheme for those who had expressed an interest in playing steel pans. This proved to be successful, and plans were in progress to develop EMPAN the name chosen by members attending practice sessions for the Steel Band which would be a new collaboration between EMCCAN, DWICA, UKTrinni and Friends.

The project was led by DWICA as it owned, stored and provided rehearsal and practice space for the group which was led by Nicola Coker of Pure Steel. EMPAN began rehearsing at Derby West Indian Community Centre every Thursday night and received support from Derby County Community Trust (DCCT), Education Learning Service (ELS) and Derby Cultural Education Partnership (DCEP). EMPAN began to perform at venues on request before the pandemic.

From 2020-22, the coronavirus pandemic stopped all development. However, the organisation will continue to explore opportunities for the growth of its own steel pan orchestra.

A Celebration of Black Heritage Across the Airwaves

In the early 1970s, two members of DWIA's post-war Windrush generation, Mr. C. McBean and Jerry Smith, negotiated with BBC Radio Derby to create a radio programme designed for and presented by Black people to meet the demands of the local African-Caribbean community. This resulted in the birth of BBC Radio Derby's 'Black Roots' programme.

Wesley Clarke was the first presenter and he was supported by a team of researchers including Pam Gabbidon and Marcela and Ken Ashley. Both Pam Gabbidon (as she was known at the time) and Yvonne Guy undertook BBC Radio training for one year in order to gain the skills necessary for broadcasting, such as interview techniques and the use of analogue tape machines and live broadcasting.

In 1979, the programme was established as a weekly broadcast which had been piloted since the early 1970s with great success. The African-Caribbean radio programme was an instant hit and has been going strong ever since.

Today, Devon Daley presents a programme aimed at Derby's Black community. The show airs every Sunday at 8pm and is a mix of Music and conversation with an African and Caribbean flavour.

Devon is passionate about the programme. "It's about bringing diversity to the airwaves and to the city. We're trying to show the best of our culture," he says. "I want to give a platform to people to talk about issues that are relevant to their lives and to celebrate our culture."

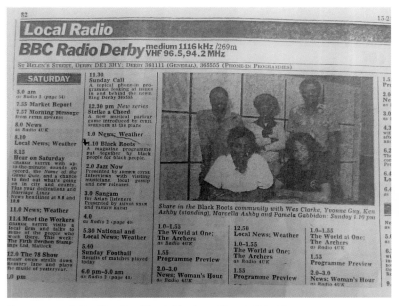

Newspaper listing for the Black Roots radio programme

Black Roots presenters Glen Wright and Yvonne Guy

The table below is a summary of DWIA participation in the development of a Black radio programme working in partnership with BBC Radio Derby

DATE	VENUE	SUMMARY FROM THE DWIA MINUTES BOOK
23.10.76	Pear Tree House	Members agreed that DWIA Chairman to be on a discussion panel on BBC Radio Derby in November regarding Race Relations.
22.4.79	Havana Club	DWIA Chairman praised the producers of BBC Radio Derby's 'Black Roots' programme which he listened to and found very interesting and informative. Mr Lee (DWIA Treasurer) suggested DWIA send a letter to BBC Radio Derby thanking them for allowing airtime for Caribbean people.
26.8.79	Havana Club	The Chairman suggested a letter should be sent to BBC Radio Derby, the four 'Black Roots' programme presenters, and support team thanking them for their support to promote DWIA's Summer Festival.
OCT 1986	DWICA	As part of DWIA's participation in the national YEAR LONG campaign Caribbean Focus 1986 (management by the Commonwealth Institute) delivered the following projects that included, Gospel concert at the Queens Hall on 10th October; Island Exhibition on 3rd-10th October at DWICA promoting Caribbean island's culture & traditions; National Sport, Business, Import & Export; Fun Run on 5th October – A charity fundraising event for the National Flood Appeal orchestrated by the Jamaica High Commission. BBC Radio Derby's 'Black Roots' presenters gave a live broadcast; Luncheon Day on 25th October at DWICA. This event captured via audio recordings old time Caribbean traditions and experiences of the post-war Windrush Generation.

Black Roots presenters

Presenter/s summary	Years
Programme launch & Broadcast: BLACK ROOTS Wesley Clarke	1970s
Yvonne Guy & Glen Wright	1981-82
Deborah Rose	1991-93
Devon Daley solo including gospel with Hopeton Gordon & Hughie Lawrence. Programme rebranded to The Devon Daley Show in 1997	1993-2002
Programme rebranded as the African Caribbean Experience presented by Devon Daley, Stephanie Hernandez, Hopeton Gordon, Bea Udeh (2002-2007)	2002-11
Devon Daley	2011-present

A Look Across the Decades

1968   Mr McKenzie forms the first Derby Caribbean Cricket Team

The owner of Charlton Taxis (Bramble Street) becomes the first African-Caribbean man to own a taxi company, corner shop and driving school

1973   DWIA cricket team affiliated and playing in Nottinghamshire & Border cricket league

Rainbow Football Team formed

1974   April – George Mighty becomes the first African-Caribbean teacher in Derby (DWICA member) teaching at Sturgess School

Hodgkinson Cafe established with DWICA member Ross Underwood and Leo Bennet

April – DWICA members established Council Advisory Service (CAS), 104 Pear Tree Road. Led at the time by Fabian Best and George Mighty and other DWICA members

1976   DWICA members start of development

Caribbean independence from Britain in the 1960s

In the 1960s, four Caribbean countries achieved independence from Britain, changing the course of their histories for ever. Jamaica, Trinidad and Tobago, Guyana and Barbados each achieved this feat in their own unique ways. Today, these four countries are proud to acknowledge the courage and determination of those who fought for their right to self-governance.

Jamaica experienced its own nationalist fervour starting in the late 1940s. Under the leadership of the Jamaica Labour Party, it made great strides towards independence. The country eventually declared independence on 6th August 1962.

In Trinidad and Tobago, the struggle for independence began in the late 1950s. As the country moved closer to self-governance, the British government passed a law in 1958 that unified the territories of Trinidad and Tobago and granted them internal self-government. After a few years of preparations, the day finally came when Trinidad and Tobago officially declared its independence on 31st August 1962.

In Guyana (formerly British Guiana), nationalist sentiment started to build in the 1940s and continued to grow as groups such as the People's Progressive Party (PPP) gained momentum and worked towards their goal of independence. In 1961, universal adult suffrage was granted and subsequently, a new constitution passed in 1962, which moved the country down the path to independence. On 26th May 1966, the Union Flag was lowered and the country was declared the independent Cooperative Republic of Guyana.

In Barbados, the first organised push for independence began in the 1950s with the Barbados Labour Party (BLP). This popular party worked to establish a foundation of solidarity and self-determination among the people of Barbados. It wasn't until 30th November 1966, that Barbados officially declared its independence from Great Britain.

work / set up Pear Tree Community Steel Band

1977/8 Credit Union formed by DWICA members Sam Lee, Bob Murray, George Mighty, Yvette Schloss, Pam Gabbidon, Monica Dean, Eric Baudeille and Cleveland Chin. First meeting held at The Chestnut Tree Pub, Portland Street, Derby

DWIA members, through fundraising and grants, purchase a set of steelpans (£485)

1979 DWICA netball team set up and playing (practice sessions at Normanton Park)

1980 Leo Bennet the first African-Caribbean youth & community worker in Derby

First issue of Derby West Indian Association & Affiliated Bodies newsletter

July – Derby Caribbean Cricket team head the Notts & Border League Premier Division 2 league with the following statistics: Played 14; won 6; lost 3; drew 5. Top Batsmen: T. Hall 424; A. James 417; D. Bell 333. Bowlers' wickets: Ces McDonald 43; Neville Black 18; Lasuad Gondell 16; Trevor Archibald 16.

July – DWIA Rainbow football team were unbeaten all season, hence Premier League Champions. Finalist in the cup match losing to Spontoon Dynamos, winners of the Derby Festival Trophy two consecutive years

9th August – DWICA Jamaica Independence Dance at Pennine Hotel. In attendance representing the Jamaica High Commission, Rt Hon McKenzie Phillip Whitehead MP and Deputy Mayor & Mayoress (Mrs Tunicliffe) Mrs Hunt (Lonsdale Travel)

September – Rainbow FC won Festival Football Completion for the 3rd

consecutive year beating Simba Youth Club (London). Homelands School won the Lonsdale Travel (inaugural year) Trophy Junior 5-a-Side Competition

2nd September – DWIA Festival at Municipal Sports Ground (Moorways) – Two Caribbean High Commissioners

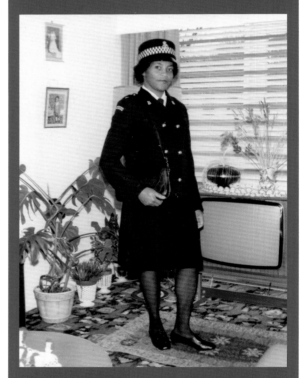

Derbyshire's first Black Special Constable

In the 1970s, Enid Francis became the first Black Special Constable to join the Derbyshire Constabulary. She was inspired to join the force following the help she received from the police when her two young sons had gone missing. The boys were found safe and well but the events left a lasting impression on her. Enid was overwhelmed by the support she received and how empathetic the officers were throughout the search.

This lasting impression led to her applying to join the Derbyshire Constabulary following an advertisement she had seen for the recruitment of Special Constables. She went through and passed all the training and served for many years.

attended, Rt Hon Ernest Peart (Jamaica) and Rt Hon. D Spooner (Guyana). Activities included stalls, floats, steelbands and sports competitions.

DWIA fundraises for the Dominica Hurricane Relief Fund with a prize draw

November – DWIA cricket team leaves for its tour of Jamaica playing local teams. Part sponsored by Lonsdale Travel & firms in Derby

29th November – DWIA cricket team leaves for its tour of Jamaica playing local teams. This was made possible through part-sponsorship from Lonsdale Travel & firms in Derby

1981   January – DWIA Saturday School at Pear Tree House Community Centre

January – Crusader FC just missed out on promotion from Division 2, Derby City League and lost out in the semi-finals of the Normanton Express Intermediate cup. Final match against King's Head draw 1-1. Clive Patterson scored for crusaders

May – Rainbow FC draw 1-1 in cup match on 17th May and lost in the replay at Derby Municipal Ground Moor Lane on 31st May

Cricket Carib team 1 - Head of Premier Division 2 Nott's & Border League losing no matches to Date (May) finished 4th place in their first season in Derby & District league

Cricket Carib team 2 - 30th May team won their first match of the season

Caribs Junior Cricket team (13yrs and under) Entered in the National Cricket Association played 3 won 3 DWIA member Bob Murray Manager

Athletics – David Marr new AA champion for Derbyshire 17.5 second 110 m hurdles World record held at the time by Renaldo Nehemiah in Zurich 1981 lowering his own WR by 0.07 seconds to *record* a new mark of 12.93

June – DWIA & Affiliated Bodies Community News, Issue 11. Key articles and information on fundraising for DWIA community / cultural centre

Caribbean independence from Britain in the 1970s

In the 1970s, the Caribbean nations of Grenada, Dominica, St Lucia and St Vincent and the Grenadines achieved independence from Britain. After centuries of exploitation under European colonial rule, the four nations achieved autonomy in a unified declaration of liberty and freedom.

Grenada was the first to take the initial steps towards self-governance. In 1967, the governments of Britain and Grenada signed an agreement which provided for internal self-government. The agreement was later implemented in 1974, paving the way for events that would lead to independence on 7th February the same year.

Dominica was officially granted independence on 3rd November 1978. Prior to this, there had been a campaign of mostly peaceful protest by the islanders seeking independence from Britain.

Leaders of the independence movement were not only instrumental in calling for the right to govern their own country, but also in ensuring that Dominica had the necessary infrastructure and legal framework to be successfully self-governed.

St Lucia gained independence on 22nd February 1979, after years of social and political agitation on the island. Like other Caribbean nations, St Lucia was under European colonial rule to some degree or another since the 16th century. Independence had been a goal pursued by many generations of St Lucians who, in 1979, finally achieved victory.

St Vincent and the Grenadines celebrated their independence on 27th October 1979. The move to independence was the culmination of many years of hard work and dedication on the part of the people who wanted to be masters of their own destiny.

1990 September – Sickle Cell & Thalassaemia support group formed. Meetings are held on a monthly basis at DWIA Centre

1991 June – West Indies cricket team visits DWICA and presents a cricket bat signed by team members

Boxer Lloyd Honeyghan (WBC, WBA & IBF welterweight champion from 1986 to 1987 and WBC welterweight champion from 1988 to 1989) visits DWICA to raise funds for University of West Indies Appeal

1992 DWICA social groups – Domino Club, Darts and social & cultural dance group, Black Jewels remain part of DWICA's list of activities

June – DWICA takes part in ITV telethon

A day with Prince Charles

As part of a nationwide tour, Prince Charles visited Derby on 27 February 1981. He engaged with members of Derby's minority communities during his visits to a local mosque, a Sikh temple, a Ukrainian community centre and the Serbian Orthodox church.

He met with members of the local African Caribbean heritage community at the Drop-in Coffee Bar where the Prince tried his hand at bar football. At the Madeley Centre's Disco Club, the "have-a-go-Prince" treated onlookers to a display of his dance skills.

Prince Charles plays bar football with Elaine Mckellar at the Drop-in Coffee Bar. Image source: Local Studies Library

At the Madeley Centre on Rose Hill Street, Prince Charles met with members of the Derby West Indian Association. He is pictured, from left to right, with Bob Murray and DWIA President, Solomon 'Ricky' Walters. Ricky arrived in England in 1956 and worked at British Celanese and British Rail before opening the Havana Club, also in 1956. The club was one of the earliest African Caribbean clubs to be established in the UK. Image source: Local Studies Library

The Prince accepts an invitation to show his moves the Disco Club. Image source: Local Studies Library

function at Swadlincote (charity event)
August – NO CARNIVAL (annual report states) as a result of funding cost for using Moorways and a lack of co-operation/support from Derby City Council. Possible new venue: Osmaston Park

1993 DWICA Domino match fixtures received for 1993
DWICA Dance Group, Black Jewels performed at Jamaica's Independence celebrations
7th August – 10th year DWICA building anniversary dance
4th September – Derby Caribbean Carnival at Normanton Park. DWICA Carnival Talent Show won by Beverley Knight who then went on to international success and recognition as an acclaimed UK R&B singer

1993 August – DWICA netball team enter city wide tournament

1994 September – DWICA hosts an Autumn Fayre

1995 May – DWIA hosts a Spring Fayre
5th August – DWICA Jamaica Independence Dinner & Dance

1996 17th May – DWICA Family Day & Book Launch of 'Lest We Forget: The Experiences of World War II West Indian Ex-Service Personnel' by Robert N. Murray (Hansib)
August - DWICA Jamaica Independence Dinner & Dance
31 August – DWICA holds Derby Caribbean Carnival at Osmaston Park

1997 DWICA change constitution to keep up with Charities Act 1993
3rd August – Jamaica's 35th Anniversary of Independence Service
9th August – Jamaica's Independence Dance Carnival
15th & 16th August – Gospel concerts

Home Secretary visits Derby

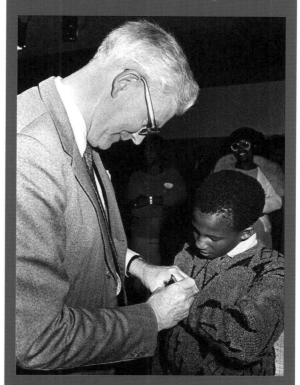

In June 1987, Britain's then Home Secretary, Douglas Hurd, visited Derby. The visit was facilitated by Derby Council for Racial Equality.

The Home Secretary met with members of Black and other minority ethnic communities at their various centres where he spoke about the work of the Home Office in dealing immigration and its legislation. He also answered questions from members of the various communities during sessions that were sometimes heated. Attendants to these meeting were most vocal in expressing their concerns and anxieties about the plight of Black and minority ethnic people in Derby and British society in general.

In a conversation with DWICA Chairman, George Mighty at the West Indian Community Centre, the Home Secretary said: "I would advise you to get all the members of your community to register for British citizenship before 31st December 1987 because the British Nationality Law is going to change beyond recognition."

23rd August – Carnival Queen Show finals

30th August – Carnival Day

29th November – DWICA's First Annual Youth Conference. Guest speaker Des Coleman, who was then a young actor on the popular BBC soap, Eastenders

2005   The Annual Youth Conference took on a national focus and had over 200 young people from across the country gathered at the Centre for the event facilitated by some outstanding Black professionals.

Caribbean independence from Britain in the 1980s

The 1980s saw two Caribbean islands achieve independence from their former colonial masters in Britain. Antigua and Barbuda and St Kitts and Nevis both achieved independence in the first half of the decade.

Antigua and Barbuda gained independence on 1st November 1981 after centuries of British colonial rule. The process of divestiture had started in 1967, when the islands were granted self-government, but it wasn't until 1981 that full sovereignty was achieved.

The process for St Kitts and Nevis spanned many decades of activism and struggle. The first move towards autonomy came in 1967 when St Kitts and Nevis were granted the status of an Associated State under the West Indies Act. This gave the two islands internal autonomy, but they were still ultimately subject to the British Crown.

In 1975, the Labour Party of St Kitts and Nevis launched a program of decolonisation and increased economic independence, but it was not until 19th September 1983 that the islands achieved full independence.

The Seven Sisters

ritain's National Health Service (NHS) was one of the institutions that provided many jobs for people arriving from the Caribbean from the late 1940s and the decades since. In the aftermath of the Second World War, the nation was suffering from severe labour shortages in many areas.

People from the Caribbean were enticed by the promise of training and the opportunity to acquire valuable experience, possibly to take back to their countries of origin in the future.

Many took up this offer of nursing positions within the NHS providing a much-needed boost to the institution. The Caribbean community in Derby also played its part, where a long line of nurses, porters and administrators have all hailed from the Caribbean.

One family that made a great contribution to the NHS in Derby was the Percy family from Kingston, Jamaica. The family's contribution began with two parents who took up roles in the NHS, followed by their seven daughters, who all trained to be nurses at the Derby Royal Infirmary.

It all began in 1955 when Donald Percy came to England. A year and a half later he sent for his wife, Irene, and his youngest son. Both parents took up roles as care assistants at the Royal Infirmary. Later, Donald spoke with the matron and told her that he had seven daughters and that they all want to become nurses. The

The percy family

Olga Marr in her early years working for the NHS

matron said that so long as the girls had at least two O level qualifications – but one in biology and the other in English – and they pass the nurses' training, she would take them on. He conveyed the news to his daughters and as soon as each one came of age, they travelled to England to undertake nurse training.

Six of the seven sisters went on to train as State Registered Nurses (SRN) at the Derby Royal Infirmary. This was quite unusual at the time since most Caribbean nurses took the lesser qualification of State Enrolled Nurse (SEN).

Lola, the eldest, trained in 1957 to become a nurse and then went to the United States after marrying. She forged a nursing career and then went into teaching the profession. Four others – Olga, Norma, Dalia and Etherine – became ward sisters in Derby. Barbara and Eunice both had long nursing careers. Etherine became a ward sister and then qualified with a degree to

become a nurse tutor in Nottingham until she retired.

The NHS owes a debt of gratitude to the women and men of the Caribbean who answered the call in the first years after the war and the decades since. However, for Olga, it came at a cost. She went on to become a midwife, but developed serious back issues through years of lifting patients when she was a nurse; she had to take early retirement.

Today, Olga and Barbara are active members of the Derby West Indian Community Association (DWICA), where they both take part in the vocational classes for the elderly. Olga has also been an important member of the DWICA management committee and represented the organisation on various external bodies such as the Police Liaison Committee and the Ethnic Minority Consultative and Advisory Forum of the Derbyshire local Health Authority (EMCAF).

DWICA Sickle Cell Anaemia and Thalassaemia Group

Early indications from among the Windrush Generation in Derby identified that local healthcare provision did not cater for the needs of Caribbean people. There was an absence of knowledge about this growing community, particularly from a cultural point of view, towards aiding patient recovery. This included the limited access to the types of food that made up the Caribbean diet.

This situation led to broader discussions among the African Caribbean community. The lack of information and access to public health services needed to be addressed, particularly where sickle cell anaemia and thalassaemia were concerned.

DWICA members lobbied and secured representation on various health bodies, such as Derbyshire Social Services Minority Consultation Panel; Community Health Council / Steering & Advisory Group; Southern Derbyshire Health Authority Ethnic minority consultative and advisory committee; and South Derbyshire Health Authority Consultation and Advisory Committee.

The aim was to improve the understanding and needs of the African Caribbean people and to convey this information to local health service decision makers.

This resulted in the establishment of the Derby Sickle Cell and Thalassaemia Support Group (DSCTSG) in 1989. The aim of this body was to provide a comprehensive service to those suffering from sickle cell anaemia and thalassaemia, and other blood disorders. It was also tasked with providing valuable information to health professionals as well as raising public awareness, knowledge and understanding.

In June 1998, the support group provided financial assistance towards hospital bills to local sickle cell patients at Derby City General hospital. And in March 1999, it sponsored a day trip to the Alton Towers theme park for young people living with a haemoglobin disorder. This was in partnership with Derby City General Hospital.

The DSCTSG also established working relationships with the Birmingham and the Nottingham branches of the Organisation for Sickle Cell Anaemia Relief (OSCAR), as well as the Sickle Cell Society, Sickle Watch and the Sickle Cell Anaemia Research Foundation in London.

The group received donations from local organisations including the Thursday Evening Ladies Group, Derby Black Ministers' Forum and Derby Church of God (7th Day) Trust.

The work carried out by DSCTSG also received recognition from the Derby South Member of Parliament, Margaret Beckett, who was also a patron of the group.

Over the years, the Derby Sickle Cell and Thalassaemia Support Group was served by the following individuals:

Mrs A F Brown - Chairperson
Ms N Hudson - Treasurer

Mrs Y. woodhouse - Secretary

Mr Mighty

Mr T. Walsh

Mr P Edwards

Mrs O Marr

Ms D Percy

Mr I Newby

Mr C Jackson

Mrs C McBean

D. Perry

W. Lloyd

J. Woodhouse

R. Gregory

A McAllister

DWICA would like to acknowledge the invaluable contribution made to the group by the late Mrs A F Brown (aka 'Flo'). Her dedication to the organisation as its Chairperson led the drive for improving public awareness, knowledge and support for sickle cell sufferers. Flo also was a well-respected DWICA committee member and took up the elected position on DWICA executive officers' group as Assistant Treasurer in the 1993.

Journey to Self-reliance

As the Windrush generation secured long-term employment in various sectors, it became possible to acquire savings, particularly towards the purchase of homes and vehicles.

For those that purchased a car, it opened up a new chapter in the "settling into UK" period whilst adding another dimension to their lives. Visiting family and friends and attending social and religious occasions, was an important aspect of life within the Caribbean heritage community. Using public transport was not always a pleasant experience. Discrimination and hostility towards members of the Black community were a regular occurrence. Therefore, owning a vehicle would help to eliminate such encounters.

As more and more vehicles were purchased by members of the Windrush generation, there was a need to have these vehicles repaired and serviced. There were those within the community who were skilled mechanics who established their own businesses to carry out such matters. They soon gained a reputation for good customer service and value for money, as well as providing employment for others.

Early models purchased include (clockwise from top left) the Ford Zephyr (early and later model), Ford Prefect, Hillman Minx, Morris Minor and Vauxhall Viva

History of the Minibus Project

The establishment of the Derby West Indian Community Centre led to an increase in the activities and services provided by the Association. These brought further opportunities as well as challenges, both locally and across its expanding network.

The Derby West Indian Community Association (DWICA) was engaged in inter-community exchange visits, and for transporting Summer School and Saturday School students to functions and for educational trips. The costs of hiring minibuses and coaches were becoming more expensive and the organisation considered the advantages of acquiring its own minibus for use by the Social Club.

The Association's President, Mr George Mighty, then embarked upon a fundraising venture in early 1997 to secure the necessary funds for the Minibus Project. Applications were made to Derby Pride, from which DWICA was awarded £11,000, and The National Lottery, from which it received £11,000. It was determined, however, that £22,000 would not be enough to purchase the vehicle that best suited the needs of the Association. Their

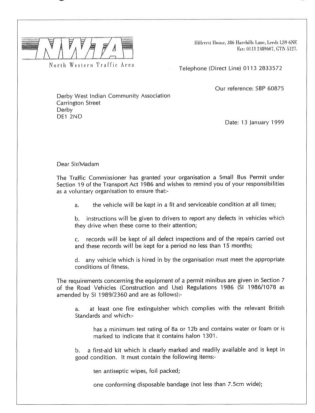

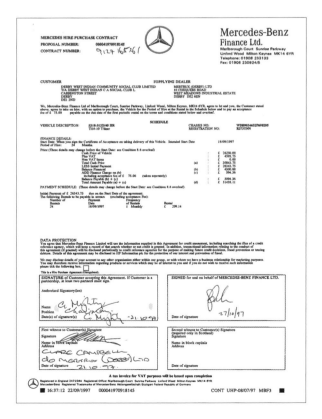

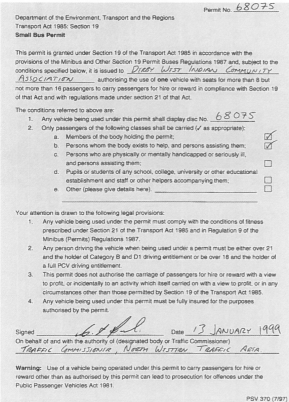

One of the most important achievements in the progress of our three-year development plan is the securing of the Centre's minibus. The bus costs approximately £32,000. It was important that we were able to buy a vehicle that would withstand the test of time. This was funded through partnership by the National Lottery Charities Board, Derby Pride and the Derby West Indian Community Association's contribution. The vehicle can transport up to 15 people and will help to enhance the links we already have with other community groups in the City and further afield. It will also be important for use on our youth project, transporting young people to various venues for social and sporting activities.

(DWICA Minibus)

minibus of choice was a Mercedes with a price tag of £31,438.

DWICA deposited £26,343.75 as a down payment and secured finance of £4,500 payable at £209.14 per month over two years from Mercedes-Benz Finance Ltd.

A few years before the vehicle was acquired, a number of restrictions were placed on minibus operators following a number of serious accidents involving minibuses, especially on school trips. DWICA's minibus had to be issued with a Special Permit by the Ministry of Transport under Section 19 of the Passenger Transport for Voluntary Groups, which restricted the use to its members and people working with members, and it could not be used for hire or fee charging. It was, therefore, restricted to the use of the association and Social Club.

The acquisition of the minibus heralded a new era in the operations of the Association and it has been a valuable asset in the development of DWICA's social, cultural and educational work.

Support for Local Football Club

The Windrush generation that came to live in Derby in the 1950s and 60s, played an enormous part in developing the city and its communities into the vibrant multi-cultural place we see today. This transition, however, wasn't without its challenges, and whilst the contributions of the many people in industry, health care and the arts are now well recognised, we should not forget the impact made by sport and particularly football.

The 1960s saw the emergence of the first predominately Black football team in the city, the Caribbean Allstars, which led the way for many more teams from minority communities to follow, including Rainbow Athletic, Crusaders and Punjab United. At its peak, many teams of young men would find their way to Darley Park, The Racecourse, Alvaston Park, Markeaton Park and other council pitches to play football.

It was without doubt one of the most powerful forces in bringing down barriers, creating new friendships and helping to establish the communities we have today.

By the early 1980s, the Caribbean Allstars and Rainbow Athletic were recognised as being two of the best amateur teams in the county, winning multiple trophies and lighting up the sports pages of the local newspapers every week. This created a wave of opportunities to join other teams, to play at higher levels based on ability, and to significantly increase integration in the sport and in the wider society. Playing football and being successful was an enormous help for those taking part, but more importantly it gave hope and a belief to many in the community that they too could be successful in whatever direction they chose. *Kenton Black*

Rainbow complete treble

Three of the key players in the Rainbow Athletic side as they bid for Derbyshire Sunday Cup and Derby Floodlit Cup success early in the New Year — Lloyd Richards, brother Cliff Richards and Dalton Taylor.

Is there an end to the Rainbow?

RAINBOW ATHLETIC, the side nobody has been able to beat or even draw against so far this season, have two tough cup-ties coming up early in the New Year.

Rainbow Athletic, mid- to late 1970s – Back row (L-R): Herby Robinson, Judson Robinson, Roddy Steadman, Charlie Walker, Dave Cooper, Euston Steadman, Irvine Scott, Delroy Davidson, Brendan Whittaker, Stan Simpson, Brenton Walker; Front row: Danny Anderson, Barrington Taylor, Roy Williams, Howard Evans, Howard Sewell.

Rainbow Athletic in the 1980s – Standing (L-R): Stan Simpson, Clifton Mitchell, Kevin Edwards, Floyd Williamson, Barrington Taylor, Dave Cooper, Brendan Whittaker, Locksley Ford; Kneeling: Cliff Richards, Charlie Walker, Gene Raymond, Denver Richards, Doulton Taylor, Lloyd Richards, Errol Burke.

RIGHT: Caribbean All-stars circa 1984 – Back row (L-R): Ton Stanley, Byron Morgan, Jimmy Campbell, Carl Wint, Grantley Edwards, Robert Whittaker, Trevor Levy, Kenton Black, Barrington Morgan, Richard Cousins; Front row: Colin Cover, Leroy Edwards, Devon Daley, Dave Powell, Malcolm Rafferty, Lloyd Wint, Des Gordon.

DWICA Football Team (late 1980s to early 1990s) – Back row (L-R): Chris Grigion, Peter John, Selvin Reid, Paddy Edwards, Andy Barrett, Wayne Briscoe; Front row: Kevin Brown, Clifton Clarke, Ricky James, Wilf Hines, Leroy Brown, Olu Operinde.

LEFT: Derby Sunday league XI representative team (circa 1982) featured key Rainbow Athletic players.

Rainbow Athletic's Brendan Whittaker in action. The striker could be one of the players to trouble Northcliffe United

Punjab must win to avoid relegation, but Rainbow manager Simpson says: "We won't be doing Punjab any favours by putting out a weakened side. It would not be fair on other clubs."

Apart from their own bid for honours, Rainbow have played a big part in leading the Derbyshire FA League to the final of the Midland Sunday Cup. Rainbow provided 14 players for the squad.

But last Sunday Derbyshire FA League slipped 3-1 in the final against Nottingham SL.

Next Wednesday, though, Rainbow must take on possibly their biggest test of the season. And a big crowd will watch them attempt to topple mighty Northcliffe.

Lloyd Richards ... two goals.

Calvin Frazer ... put

Rainbow come good at just right time

HOLDERS Rainbow Athletic had to come from 2-0 down to beat Derbyshire Police in the semi-finals of the Derbyshire FA League Premier Cup.

Police swept into a two goals lead through Bircumshaw and Bestwick. They held that advantage until half-time, but then Rainbow hit back to force extra time.

Two goals in the extra period eventually steered Rainbow through and it was a relief after a recent bad run. Rainbow have set such a tremendously high standard in recent seasons it is a shock when they have a poor run as they have recently, but the win against Police will give them a boost.

Lloyd Richards and Barry Taylor scored two goals apiece for Rainbow.

In the final, Rainbow will take on Arkwright United, who edged through 1-0 against AFC Erewash.

A second-half goal by John Kelly earned Arkwright victory in a hard-fought match.

Lloyd Richards ... two goals for Rainbow.

Support for Local Cricket Club

Trophy presentation to the victorious Crusaders team

DERBY & DISTRICT

Division 1

Crusaders v A. Magna

CRUSADERS

Brevitt b Kirkland	15
Forrester c Perry b Upton	7
Cooper not out	82
Smith b Kirkland	10
Edwards b Kirkland	5
Francie (G) b Kirkland	12
Robinson retired	15
Francis (M) b Kirkland	31
Francis (A) not out	3
Extras	22
Total (6 wkts)	**202**

Bowling: Upton 8-0-29-1, Marsh 7-1-50-0, Kirkland 15-4-54-5, Perry (A) 6-0-25-0, Bird 4-0-31-0.

APPLEBY MAGNA

Timbrell c Newman b Smith	5
Reading b Smith	31
Perry b Smith	5
Kirkland c Francis (K) b Smith	0
Mitchell c Cooper b Smith	2
Upton b Smith	4
Redfern b Smith	6
Ridgway not out	0
Marsh b Francis (M) 0	Birr
d b Smith	0
Vickers c Edwards b Smith	0
Extras	17
Total	**70**

Bowling: Edwards 6-2-15-0, Francis (M) 4-1-4-1, Smith 8.4-2-23-9, Francis (K) 6-1-18-0.

Crusaders won by 132 runs

APPLEBY put Crusaders in. Brevitt started brightly for Crusaders but the introduction of Kirkland soon saw wickets falling. It took a good innings from V. Cooper (82*) and M. Francis (31) to rescue Crusaders and reach 202 for 6. Appleby's reply was stubborn at the start, with Reading batting well but Smith made up for his failure with the bat to destroy Appleby, ending with impresive figures of 9-23.

Welcoming Sir Garfield 'Garry' Sobers to Derby: (L-R) Len Shillingford, Garry Sobers, Nelson Katachi and Crusader cricket team member, Victor Smith at Derby station on 13 September 1994.

Autographed photo of Garry Sobers in action

Back row includes: Michael Francis, Garry Francis, Albert Hutchinson and Kevin Francis; front row (L-R): Tony Newman, Vic Smith, Vernal Cooper, Mike Dale and Philip Cooper

Michael Holding signs for Derbyshire County Cricket Club in 1983.
Photo: Derby Evening Telegraph

Members of the West Indies Cricket team and local Derby people: (L-R) Joel Garner, Michael Holding, Stan Jordan, Viv Richards and Ses McDonald

ABOVE: Victor Smith, left, with West Indies cricket legend Viv Richards at Derbyshire cricket ground

LEFT – Back row (L-R): Garry Francis, Abslem Robinson, Tony Newman, Delroy Forrester and Barry Thomas; front row: Clem Nichols, Vernal Cooper, Vic Smith, Mick Dale and Danny Brevett

Charles Ollivierre (1876-1949)

In 1901, Charles Ollivierre became the first Black West Indian to play for an English county cricket team. He played in 114 first-class matches for Derbyshire until 1907 and scored a total of 4,830 runs. His highest match score was 321 runs against Essex in 1904. It has only been exceeded once in the county's history and was a Derbyshire record for over 100 years.

Michael Holding

One of the greatest – and fastest – bowlers ever to play cricket, Jamaican-born Michael Holding joined Derbyshire from 1983 until 1989. He took 249 Test match wickets for the West Indies and played in 178 matches for Derbyshire, where he took 378 wickets – including a then world One Day record of 8-21 against Sussex in 1988.

Devon Malcolm

Malcolm was born in Jamaica but Derbyshire discovered him bowling fast in the Yorkshire League for Sheffield United in the early 1980s. A bowler of raw pace, he was carefully managed by Derbyshire's captain and coach throughout the 1980s, as he developed into a magnificent match-winner, not just for Derbyshire, but also for England, for whom he took 9-57 against South Africa at The Oval in 1994. In 289 matches for Derbyshire he took 753 wickets. He played 40 Test matches for England.

LOUIS'S GOLD MEDAL GIFT TO TOWN

Local newspaper coverage of Derby's Louis Martin presenting one of his Commonwealth Games gold medals to Derby Town Council

AN UNUSUAL gift was made to Derby Town Council yesterday when Louis Martin, Derby's famed international weightlifter, presented one of his gold medals won at the Commonwealth Games in Perth in 1962, to the town.

Louis said that having retired, he considered his career a successful one through the help he had received from the Council and the people of Derby who had supported him.

"I started here and I end here," said Louis, who at the age of 33 announced his retirement from international weightlifting after the Commonwealth Games in Edinburgh this year.

"As a passing gesture, I would like to donate this 1962 Commonwealth gold medal to the town," he continued.

TO INSPIRE

"I would like it to go into the Museum so that youngsters can see it and it might inspire them sportswise," he added.

The Mayor of Derby, Alderman Miss M. E. Grimwood-Taylor (pictured receiving the gift) said that the whole town was proud that Mr. Louis Martin was one of their citizens.

"In 15 years he has done an enormous amount of work particularly for the youngsters, and I sure they will go flocking to the Museum," she said.

The motion that the Council accept the medal was passed unanimously, and Louis, his wife Ann, and son Louis, junior (three next month) left the Council chamber to standing applause.

The medal is one of three Commonwealth gold medals he won in his career as a midheavyweightlifter. He has also won an Olympic silver medal and bronze medal, has been four times world champion, and British champion 12 times.

LOUIS TO PRESENT GAMES MEDAL TO TOWN

DERBY'S famous international weightlifter, Louis Martin, is to present one of his Commonwealth medals to Derby as a token of thanks for the support he has received from the Town Council and people of the borough.

Arrangements are being made for the presentation to take place at a meeting of the Town Council on October 7.

Louis announced his intention at an informal reception given by the Mayor of Derby, Alderman Miss M. E. Grimwood-Taylor, at the Council House last night. The reception was held in his honour following Louis's success in winning a gold medal at the recent Commonwealth Games at Edinburgh.

PICTURED is the Mayor examining the gold medal won by Louis. Louis has intimated that his gift to the town would probably be a gold medal. Standing at left in picture is Mrs. Martin next to whom is the Mayoress, Miss Elizabeth Garnett.

CROWN DERBY

The Mayor presented Louis with a piece of Royal Crown Derby china on behalf of the townspeople. She said how pleased and proud the people of Derby were that he had given so much to the town.

The Mayoress presented a bouquet to Mrs. Martin.

Responding, Louis recalled that he had attended a number of similar receptions at the Council House.

"I think this will most probably be my last in this capacity, as I am thinking of retiring from the international scene," he said.

"I am getting older and cannot get about so much!"

He expressed thanks to his coach, Mr. P. J. Mann, and to Mr. F. Constable, Director of Parks, for providing him with facilities for training.

Derby Evening Telegraph

DWICA Domino Club

The game of dominoes is popular throughout the Caribbean and has been so since the 19th century. The Caribbean heritage community in Derby recognised that this important aspect of Caribbean culture was something not to be overlooked.

Derby West Indian Community Association (DWICA) records show that at a management meeting in October 1975, held at Pear Tree House, the newly-formed team received positive feedback from members and would be represented at future DWICA meetings.

By February 1976, DWICA had organised its first dominoes tournament and had invited teams from across the Midlands. The organisation later received a letter from the Nottingham & District West Indian National Association congratulating them on a successful dominoes tournament.

A typical domino club gathering

When DWICA finally got its own building in July 1981, dominoes attracted more people to come to the centre to play the game. The popularity of dominoes soon evolved into a week-day and weekend activity.

From 1985 to 1995, DWICA planned home and away matches as part of the social calendar. Home matches were long days starting with all the pre-match duties, then providing refreshments, including a hot Caribbean meal. Once the tournament finished, the day's entertainment would continue with an evening of music and dance.

Throughout the decade, the DWICA dominoes team travelled to venues across the UK, including Luton, Preston, West Bromwich, Wolverhampton, Birmingham, Sheffield and Gloucester.

Away matches also presented an opportunity for DWICA members to visit new places, as well as to make new friends or establish links with

The Hilda Douce Memorial Cup is presented by the Derby West Indian Association Dominoes Team

other members of Britain's Caribbean heritage communities.

In 1995, DWICA established its women's dominoes team. Mondays were designated as 'Ladies Dominoes Club Night' and the women's team took part in home and away tournaments. The team was very successful and defeated most of the teams it faced.

DWICA also prides itself on playing host to many dominoes tournaments which attracted teams from across the region.

In November 2013, in response to the national campaign to raise funds in the aftermath of the typhoon in the Philippines, the DWICA dominoes teams and the DWICA membership raised £1440 for the Philippines Typhoon Appeal Disasters Emergency Committee.

During the coronavirus pandemic, all activities at the centre were ceased until the lockdown status across the UK had been lifted. A weekly 'Games Night' has been re-established and includes dominoes and darts as well as the playing of other board games.

DWICA would like to acknowledge the work of the late Mrs Hilda Douce. She was a key member of the Association and volunteer who also established the DWICA dominoes teams. A trophy and competition in her name was created as part of DWICA's dominoes legacy.

A beloved Caribbean tradition

Dominoes has been played throughout the Caribbean since the 19th century. This ancient and classic game is enjoyed by people of all ages and backgrounds, and is an important aspect of Caribbean culture, where it is played in homes, streets, bars and other social gatherings.

The origins of the game date back to 12th century China, since when it quickly spread throughout Europe and eventually to the Caribbean.

In the Caribbean, dominoes is a popular social pastime and is often played in groups, and at parties and gatherings. It is also played competitively among local teams as well as across the Caribbean region.

Caribbean heritage communities across the UK have also maintained this much-loved tradition by playing for fun as well as creating their own teams and leagues.

DWICA Darts Team

I n 1984, DWICA hosted an indoor multi-sports championship at the centre which consisted of darts, dominoes, pool and table tennis. The championship concluded with an awards presentation sponsored by local company Lonsdale Travel. The event was a success because of the time and commitment of Mr Vincent Sewell.

It was from this inaugural event that the DWICA darts team was established. It became involved in the city-wide darts league and achieved a second place position in the 1985 league table. The darts team went on to greater success the following year and finished top of the Derby Darts League. They were again crowned league winners in 1988, and in 1989 they won the Derby League Championship.

The DWICA community centre also gained a reputation as an ideal venue for darts tournaments and other indoor events. Games nights and social evenings were well attended and friendly occasions. Along with darts events, the community centre hosted dominoes and indoor bowls competitions.

All of these events were made successful through the hard work and dedication of volunteers, players and supporters. Unsung heroes include the following: Gilbert "Gilly" Williamson, Myra Williamson, Cllr Harold Cox, Lloyd George Hudson, Mr and Mrs Turner, Mr and Mrs Bryan, May Bryant, Joyce Mitchell, Gloria Yorke, Egerton Perry and Burchell Davidson.

Playing darts at the community centre

Derby City Council's Community Darts Tournament trophy

Derby Black Business Agency

During the 1980s, the Derby West Indian Community Association recognised that there was a need to explore possibility of having a business support system for local Black businesses. This was in keeping with the sentiments expressed by the management committee regarding the setting up of Credit Union.

There were a number of fledging businesses that needed help to develop and grow. These businesses were established up by members of the Caribbean heritage community who are now regarded as the Windrush Generation.

In March 1987, DWICA invited local Black businesses and other interested parties to attend a meeting to discuss the setting up of a Black Business Agency.

Working in partnership with Derby City and Derbyshire County Councils, the management submitted an application to the Department of the Environment which resulted in the city of Derby gaining limited inner area status and given financial resources of £1 million.

DWICA then secured funding from Derby's Inner Area Programme to commission Ryegate Management Consultants, based in Sheffield, to produce a study to examine the problems faced by local African Caribbean businesses and prospective businesses and entrepreneurs, and to develop a plan that will facilitate an increase in the number, turnover, profitability and employment of Black-owned and managed companies in Derby.

The study commenced in July and was completed in October 1988 and a full report produced for the Black Business Steering Group (the management team leading the project).

As part of DWICA heritage and legacy commitment to make historical information available to the public, the report "Derby Black Businesses Research Project" (along with other commissioned or academic reports) are housed in Derbyshire Records Office (in Matlock) for future generations to use, such as for academic research. The information used has been taken from the commissioned report which gives some context of the time and the activities of local African Caribbean businesses.

It should be noted that there were other businesses that were not in the sample used for the survey, but they are also included in the lists.

African Caribbean businesses that took part in the survey

TYPE OF BUSINESSES	No	Main Products
Hairdressing & Barbers	6	Hairdressing services
Building & Joining (construction)	4	Services and joinery products
Public House / night clubs	4	Alcoholic & soft beverages foods & snacks

Retail Household shops	3	Household goods
Garage mechanics	3	Services,
Electrical & home appliances	3	Services
Taxi services	2	Services
Motor repairs (bodywork)	2	Services
Video shops	2	Video purchase / rental Services
Retail leather shops	1	Handbags & Hats etc,
Afro-Caribbean artefacts	1	Jewellery pictures etc.
Knitwear designs	1	knitwear
Record shops	1	Music cassette tapes / records
Central heating / engineering	1	Services
Landscape / gardening scape	1	Services, ceramics, plants
Retail pharmacy	1	Medicine and toiletries
Solicitor	1	Legal services
Financial consultant	1	Financial consultancy
Driving school	1	Tuition Services

Black Businesses in Derby by Year

BEFORE 1980	5
1980 - 1982	3
1983 1985	13
1986 – 1987	17

Staff employed

Type of employment	Staffing no	Number of employees
Full time	1-5	37
	11-25	1
Part time	1-5	14
	6-10	1

The study highlighted the barriers to Black businesses in Derby at that time as:

- Lack of access to finances, such as company loans from the banks
- Lack of suitable advisory services
- Cash flow difficulties
- Operating costs
- Lack of business experience in Derby

At the time (1988) the following companies were recognised as African Caribbean businesses trading in Derby:

Company name	Company address
Active hair design	27 Macklin St
Afro- Caribbean Arts & Crafts	85 Glengarry Rd
Bayero	339 Normanton Rd
Blake's Hairstyling	24 Grosvenor St
Z.M. Burrel Electrics	87 Empress Rd.
Cable Cars	228 Osmaston Rd
Carib Club	228 Osmaston Rd
Caror Lumlell	32 Lamp brief St (off Cambridge St)
The Dial	Willow Row
Dixon & Nelson Builders	147 Crewe St 213 St Thomas's Rd.
Derby Cars	121a Nuns St
David D. Coucenco	320 Normanton Rd
Fiona M Fabrics	203c Upper dale Rd
L.G. Forbes Ltd	147 Peartree Rd.
M. Fox Builders & Contractor	153 Almond St
Hamilton's Joinery & Carpentry	152 Portland St
Joe's garage	3 Princes St Industrial Unit
Lewis Gordon Associates	55 Porter Rd
P.A. Murfin Landscape Design & Construction	20 Arkle Green
Nation Records	58a Rosehill St
P. Noble	76 Yero dale St
Nottingham Homecare	4-5 Abbots Hill
Chambers	60b Upper Parliament St (Nottingham)
Ocean Electric Services	206 Burton Rd
Pear Tree Inn	155 St Thomas Rd
Rosemary's	226 Eagle Centre Market
Soft touch Designer Knitwear by Marvin	12 Wheeldon Ave / 44 frigate
Stax Motors	Upper dale Rd
Sunglow heating	44 Friargate
Timic Motors	84 Carrington St
Tom's Hair & Beauty Care	229 Normanton Rd
T.S Builders	175 Almond St
T.V.F.M.	63 Peartree Rd
Unique hair	Peartree Rd
Vale Street garage	83 Vale St
Velma unisex hair Salon	106 Dale Rd
Rupert Wisdom Photography	104 Dale Rd

Additional companies not included in the survey

Company name	Type of business	Company address
Baldwin Insurance	Insurance services	97 Carrington Crescent
Big Removals	Removals	86 Violet St

Burrel Electrical	Electrical contractor	87 Empress Rd
Culture Studio	(Sound system)	108 Northumberland St
N.A Edwards	Painter & Decorator	36 Renals St
Lonsdale travel ltd	(Travel & leisure consultant)	346 Normanton Rd
Prestigious Cleaning Derby ltd	Commercial building Contract cleaners	42 Keldholme Lane
Ken Reid	(Trailor)	Peartree Crescent
Harry Stanley	Painter & Decorator	91 Warner St
Mr Wright	Road transport Haulage contractor	61 Mill Hill Lane
L. Ole (Sunshine	supermarket	Bainbridge Street

The study produced four main recommendations

1. A Black Business Enterprise Agency in Derby as a catalyst for Black business development. The agency should be a partnership between:

- The African Caribbean community
- Derby City Council
- Derbyshire County Council
- The Home Office
- Department of the Environment
- The Department of Employment
- Regional enterprise unit and the private sector

2. The setting up of financial assistance schemes for Black businesses administered by the proposed agency.

3. Secure training provider status / accreditation specialising in the development of specific training programs for existing and potential Black entrepreneurs

4. Supporting the development of a managed workspace as a community-led self-help project.

The Black Business Agency (BBA) then employed a Chief Executive Officer (CEO) to work with local businesses to improve the opportunities for growth (new customers) and development (products, services, equipment and staff).

One of the BBA's business support functions was to test the viability of new local business ideas (at the "incubator" stage) against a set of business principles used by the banks when considering loans to new and small businesses. From this process it gave such businesses the confidence to understand the business sector in relation to their business venture.

In addition, it gave small loans to businesses to assist through the incubator business development stages.

The work of the BBA received city-wide recognition and as such the business support work merged with a wider community business agency which would then take on the identity of the **Derby Ethnic Minority Business Agency**.

DWICA members and volunteers devoted many hours towards the development of the BBA, in particular, Milton Crosdale (Chairman), Willitz Gabbidon (Secretary), Lloyd Newby (Treasurer), Garnet Parris (CEO), George Mighty, Melvin Guy, Oslen Letford and Verna Williams.

The Havana Night Club

Established in 1965 by Solomon 'Ricky' Walters, the Havana Club was located in Uttoxeter Old Road and soon became a popular venue for Derby's African Caribbean community.

Ricky migrated to England in 1956 and worked at British Celanese for a short period before moving to British Rail.

The club was renowned as a safe and friendly environment offering music and dance, and was a place where African Caribbean people could relax and enjoy themselves in comfort. Its popularity attracted people from across the country and ran for more than thirty years.

Caribbean Focus 1986

Following the success of the festival of Sri Lanka in 1981 and of India in 1982 the Commonwealth Institute decided to embark on a programme of bi-annual regional focuses. The first of these focuses was "Africa Africa" in 1984. The next featured the Caribbean in 1986 followed by the Pacific in 1988.

Earlier festivals and focuses include "key events" on education, cultural, artistic, economic, social and religious history, and development of the particular area. The same format was adopted for Caribbean focus 1986.

To ensure an effective national project management structure was in place, the Commonwealth Institute created a national body called Caribbean Focus 1986, British Committee. This was a national committee that met on a regular basis and was chaired by Mr Ivo de Souza, former Jamaica High Commissioner. It was attended by over twenty-five delegates representing major cities in England and Wales, including Derby. The national body's aim was to work in collaboration with initiatives from the Caribbean and participating cities and encourage the establishment of regional Caribbean Focus committees which would be responsible for developing and delivering a programme of activities reflecting the key events linked to the national body.

Regional Caribbean focus committees were then established to plan a year-long programme of activities to celebrate the Caribbean nations through educational activities. Due to late funding, Derby's regional committee had twelve members and met on a monthly basis to plan a programme of activities. As part of DWICA's strategic networking, it maintained a presence at the national level by regularly attending Caribbean Focus 1986 British Committee meetings. As a result, the national body accepted Derby's programme of activities as a positive contribution to the national programme. Derby's programme of activities included:

- Church Service on Saturday 24th September at Derby Cathedral in collaboration with Derby Afro Caribbean Council of Churches. This event gave members of various churches the opportunity to deliver comforting and inspiring words from local adult and young people's choirs, and testimonies. The guest of honour was The Mayor and Mayoress of Derby.

- Gospel concert on Friday 10th October at Queens Hall (London Road), in partnership with Derby Council of Churches choirs from Leeds, Luton, Northampton and Derby, performed to a well-attended event.

- Island exhibition on Friday 3-10 October at DWICA. In partnership with CAS Derby Multi cultural centre and the Caribbean Gallery (London) promoted an educational project

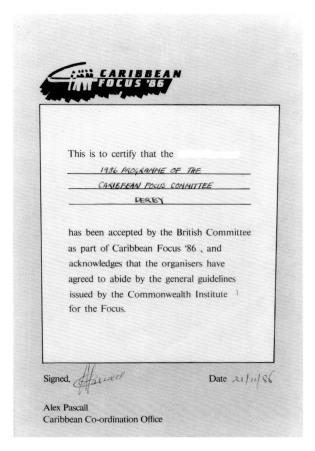

This is to certify that the

1986 PROGRAMME OF THE

CARIBBEAN FOCUS COMMITTEE

DERBY

has been accepted by the British Committee as part of Caribbean Focus '86 , and acknowledges that the organisers have agreed to abide by the general guidelines issued by the Commonwealth Institute for the Focus.

Signed, _____   Date 21/11/86

Alex Pascall
Caribbean Co-ordination Office

to educate school children and the general public about Caribbean people's islands and traditions, currency, national sport and business. This exhibition complemented the Caribbean Express train that came to Derby Train Station as part of the Caribbean Focus 1986 Commonwealth Institute national initiative.

- 5km sponsored Fun Run on Sunday 19th October at DWICA. A charity fundraising event for the National Flood Appeal orchestrated by the Jamaica High Commission. BBC Radio Derby's Black Roots Caribbean programme promoted the Appeal a week before on Sunday 5th October and the programme's radio presenters attended the event on the day and recorded segments of the event. It should be noted that BBC Radio Derby Black Roots presenters made Caribbean Focus 86 a monthly article that gave updates on forthcoming activities, and on matters relating to the Caribbean. The charity fun run raised £50 which was then added to the £500 raised by the generosity of the Derby community, and duly forwarded to the Jamaica High Commission.

- Luncheon Day on 25th October at DWICA. This event in partnership with Chronicle of Minority Arts (CHROMA Nottingham) was designed to capture the old time Caribbean traditions and experiences, including Caribbean food. Volunteers recorded audio interviews and testimonies of the post-World War 2 first generation of the Caribbean community in Derby.

Events and Celebrations

Early records show that at a management meeting on Thursday 15th February 1962 at 25 Crewe Street (DWIA Treasurer's home) the organisation agreed to change the date and name for the annual event from 15th June to 3rd August to coincide with Jamaica's independence anniversary, and the name of the event to 'Jamaica Independence Dinner and Dance' instead of 'Federation Dance'.

This event was DWIA's first big event which proved to be a success and as such the birth of DWICA's Jamaica Independence Dinner & Dance, which would be held in August.

Such annual events would be held at various premier venues of the day such as Tiffany's, now known as the Locarno Ballroom, the Pennine Hotel, Co-op, and the Trocadero. In attendance were many dignitaries such as Caribbean high commissioners, UK MPs, local councillors and celebrities. The dinner provided is a Caribbean menu and the entertainment is generally from live performances and music by one of the Windrush generation's DJs, such as the well-known Papa Steel.

DWICA also planned the organisation's annual Christmas Dinner & Dance held in December. Other social events are also organised for volunteers that give their time, expertise and skills to aid the organisation's community development projects, such as the Derby Caribbean Carnival, Covid Kitchen and weekly social gatherings, among others.

Members in attendance at the Derby West Indian Community Centre on the occasion of the visit by Jamaica's Governor General and Jamaica's High Commissioner in 1998

Visit by Jamaica's Governor-General, Sir Howard Cooke (left), and Jamaica's High Commissioner to the UK, Derick Heaven, in 1998

Commemorative plaque presented to the Jamaica's Governor General

Mr Solomon Walters, left, and members at the buffett table on the occasion of the visit by Jamaica's Governor General and High Commissioner in 1998

60th Anniversary Celebration

On 21st June 2015, a lunch was held to celebrate the 60th anniversary of the founding of the Derby West Indian Community Association. Mr Charles Hill (pictured right), who was the Vice President of DWIA in 1961 and one of the Association's founder members in 1955, attended the event as a special guest.

Mr Hill's son-in-law gave a speech on his behalf and highlighted the importance of the Association to continue to unite and to support everyone in the West Indian community. He also acknowledged the on-going work of DWICA and its value to the community.

As Chair of the Association, George Mighty addressed the audience of around 70 guests and provided an insight into DWICA's history over the years.

The event was also an opportunity for old friends to meet and reminisce and to enjoy a programme of entertainment that included singing, poetry-reading, story-telling and comedy.

Black History Month

In October 2019, a Carnival Art Exhibition was held entitled "Man behind the Mask". This was put on by a young Derby artist, Samantha Hudson, who also held an exhibition at the Quad. In October 2020, a four-week exhibition was held at the centre which highlighted weekly sub-exhibitions of Caribbean heritage and the work done by the organisation over the years.

Visit by Jamaica's High Commissioner

On 11th September 2019, the Jamaican High Commissioner, His Excellency Seth George Ramocan, visited the Derby West Indian Community Centre. His trip to Derby also included visits to a number of locations, including one to Derby City Council where he met with the Mayor of Derby, Councillor Frank Harwood.

At St Benedict's School, he met with the headteacher and a number of students who were of West Indian heritage.

The High Commissioner also visited Derbyshire Constabulary Headquarters where he met with the Police and Crime Commissioner for Derbyshire, Hardyal Dhindsa, the Chief Constable, Peter Goodman, and members of staff.

An evening reception was later held at the community centre in his honour which also provided an opportunity for the community to meet and greet the High Commissioner and members of his entourage.

Jamaica's High Commissioner to the UK and DWICA Chairman with the Mayor of Derby, Frank Harwood, in 2019

During his visit to Derby in 2019, Jamaica's High Commissioner to the UK, Seth George Ramocan, accompanied DWICA Chairman, George Mighty on a visit to Saint Benedict Catholic Voluntary Academy

Visit by Jamaica's High Commissioner to the UK, Seth George Ramocan, in 2019. He is pictured with DWICA Chairman, George Mighty.

Jamaica's High Commissioner to the UK, Seth George Ramocan (centre) is flanked by Chief Constable, Peter Goodman (left) and Police and Crime Commissioner for Derbyshire, Hardyal Dhindsa (right). DWICA Chairman, George Mighty (front, second from right) is pictured with (from far left to right) Jamaica High Commission Community Relations Officer, Viviene Siva, Berimma Sankofa and Angella Mighty of DWICA and (far right) Nezrine Hudson of DWICA.

Annual Christmas Dinner

Christmas dinner and celebrations took place on 7th December 2019, in which over 40 people were in attendance. Based on feedback and the success of the previous year a new format was adopted, making it a more relaxed occasion. A buffet-style menu of Caribbean dishes was available. The Sheba Soul Ensemble, also known as Black Sisters on the Move, provided the entertainment for the evening. The evening also included performances by solo artists, storytelling and poetry-reading.

Gospel Event

On 22nd February 2020, there was a gospel event with musical performances by various artists, including gospel choir renditions with music by Orett Lawrence. The event was a great success and was thoroughly enjoyed by all those in attendance.

Youth Conference

In 2019, the Youth Conference made a return with the theme '*Striving Towards Success*'. This took place on Saturday 6th July and had a great response from the young people and wider members of the community. The purpose of this event was to inspire and encourage young people within the Derby community and show the number of opportunities young Black people have in Derby.

40 Years of DWICA Community/Cultural Centre

On 31st July 2022, DWICA celebrated the 40th anniversary of the Derby West Indian Community/Cultural Centre. Old VHS and video footage of the centre from 1992 to 2022 was shown to remind members and visitors of all that has happened at the centre since it was built in 1982. The niece of the Association's former President/Chairman, Mr Solomon 'Ricky' Walter, attended the celebration. She had contacted the centre after learning about the organisation's project, The Centre That Power the Road exhibition at Derby Museum and Art Gallery and her uncle's involvement.

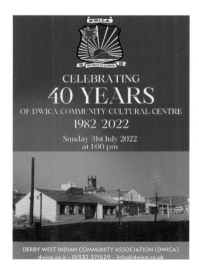

Windrush Celebrations

The Windrush Thanksgiving Service is a part of the National Windrush Day events. The Derby West Indian Community Association (DWICA) in conjunction with the Assemblies of the First-Born Holy Trinity Church held its fourth Service of Thanksgiving for the Windrush generation on 25th June 2023. The Thanksgiving Service is an opportunity to acknowledge both past and present members of the Windrush generation. This was followed by a social gathering which provided an opportunity for discussions and reflections by those wishing to share their Windrush experiences.

DWICA's Angella Mighty and Nezrine Hudson (left) and guests at the Windrush Tranksgiving Service and Celebration event, right

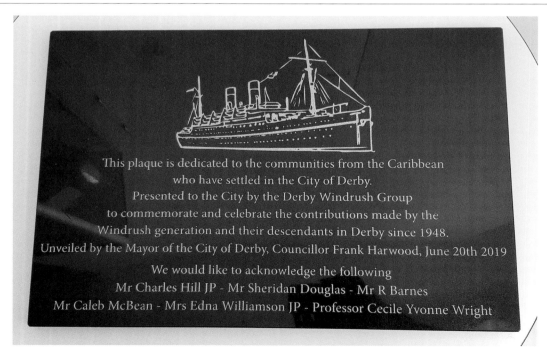

Plaque acknowledging the contribution made to Derby by members of the Caribbean community

Days Out and Excursions

Visiting places of interest was an integral part of socialising amongst DWIA members as well as getting to know other parts of the country. Early visits included day-trips to Llandudno in Wales, in June 1963 and to Skegness in August 1963. Also, a trip to Scarborough on Whit Sunday in May 1965, Blackpool Illuminations in October 1966 and to Southport in Merseyside in June 1968.

DWIA went on to plan further family annual trips to places of interest such as sightseeing in London in June 1972, and a visit to Morecombe in August 1973. Out of town social nights to other African Caribbean venues were also planned, including to the Bamboo Club in Bristol in August 1975.

Over the years DWICA has organised visits to the film set of Coronation Street, one of the country's longest running television soaps. As the organisation grew so did its social and recreational trips to cities. This was demonstrated by visiting other African Caribbean community centres across the country to play in dominoes matches. These included visits to Luton, Preston, Huddersfield, West Bromwich, Wolverhampton, Birmingham, Sheffield, High Wycombe, Walsall and Gloucester.

These occasions involved the playing of various dominoes matches and competitions followed by a social night of music and dance.

Responding to demands, further day trips included Blackpool Pleasure Beach and a number of parks which were attended by all age groups. These visits were usually organised by DWICA's summer school annual big trip activity.

In addition, further trips were planned during DWICA's carnival troupe annual tour season from June to August. Regular tours included to the four Carnivals of East Midlands Caribbean Carnival Arts Network - Derby, Nottingham, Leicester and Northampton. The troupe also visited Leeds West Indian Carnival and has done so for over 25 years.

Representation on External Bodies

Before the establishment of the Derby West Indian Association (DWIA), founder members provided social, educational and employment advice and representation to members of the local Caribbean community. This representation was undocumented, but with DWIA established as a constituted organisation, it became easier to keep track of who was representing the community in meetings and on external bodies. Over the years, this has had a positive impact and improved community cohesion. DWIA has become a recognised Caribbean community organisation, earning the respect of both central and local government, who turn to it when undertaking research into community services and project initiatives.

The timeline below highlights some of DWICA early key external strategic networking undertaken since 1961:

1961-1971

- Migrant Services meeting (London)
- Community meeting (Wirksworth)
- Jamaica Netball Team social gathering (London)
- West Indies cricket team charity cricket match at Oval Cricket ground (London)
- Jamaica Independence celebration (Manchester)
- DWIA donated £10 and 10 shillings to families of three policemen killed in the line of duty (London)

- DWIA sends two (2) representatives to memorial service for the late Prime Minister of Jamaica Rt Hon Sir Donald Sangster (London)
- Mr Hill agrees to be DWIA representative on matters relating to the police (Derbyshire)
- DWIA agrees to donate 25 guineas to "Sir Alexander Bustamante Foundation Scholarship via the Jamaica High Commission (London)
- Selected members met Sir Lawrence Lindo Jamaica High Commissioner at the Midland Hotel (Derby)
- Meeting with Litchfield Theological College, and meet the young vicars (Derby)
- Meeting with the Welfare Officer to the West Midlands branch of the JA High Commission (Birmingham)
- Attend Meetings at Council for Community Relations 0ffices (CCR) in (Derby)
- DWIA member on Pear Tree House management committee (Derby)
- Met the new Jamaica High Commission Minister of Trade and Industry (London)
- Give presentation to Garden Fete event (Kedleston)
- A donate £20 given to the Newly formed football club called "Rainbow Athletic Club" (Derby)
- Attend Derby Trades Union Council (TUC) meetings

1972-1984

- Attend as DWIA representative for Derby Council for Community Relations (DCCR) key issue "black school leavers being turned down for jobs". The DWICA Chairman agreed to take up the matter with Council for Community Relations.

- Invitation to participate in Provost of Derby Multicultural Arts & Craft exhibition (Derby)
- DWIA staff meeting with Derby Education Office and secures an agreement to allow unemployed young West Indian people to go to college for five days instead of three without it affecting or losing their unemployment benefit – (Derby)
- DWIA Chairman attends a discussion panel on BBC radio Derby regarding Race Relations (Derby)
- DWIA Chairman reports to members on the meeting with the Queen at Buckingham Place (this elevated DWIA status on a national level)
- UK Immigrant Advisory Service annual conference - (Hartford)
- Supporting national umbrella organisation to form a nationwide organisation of all Jamaican organisation in the UK to improve strength and effectiveness and support to all members to address social issues (spearheaded by Manchester and London)
- Support Derbyshire Police Authority and young people improve community understanding / relations / community cohesion
- DWIA Chairman met police staff at the police training centre to discuss improving community relations
- DWIA sits on Community Advisory Service (CAS) management committee (Derby)
- Represent DWIA at Derby Trades Council inviting DWIA to their annual dance
- Chairman asked for support on the matter of equal opportunities which will be an agenda item at October 1977 Derby Trade Council meeting
- DWIA management gave a presentation to members in November 1977 of the changes the government is planning for immigrants holding British passports
- Letter from the Chancellor of the Exchequer, and The Department of Health & Social Security acknowledging DWIA letters. In addition, DWIA receive a Letter from Chancellor of the Exchequer's Private Secretary Mr. Keith Howe stating the proposal to phase out child tax allowance would be suspended until further notice.
- The national body Community Relation Equality (CRE) invited DWIA representative to a two-day conference in September 1978 (London)
- CRE Birmingham inviting DWIA to attend a conference for BME groups in the East Midlands to develop a meaningful and effective liaison between CRE and minority groups in the area in June 1978 (Leicester)
- Members invited and agreed to meet Leicester Community Association in August 1978
- CRC Birmingham invites DWIA to send two representatives to a conference in October (Leicester)
- CAS invites DWIA to send one or two representatives to a meeting to discuss having a law centre in Derby (October 1978)
- DWIA hosted a meeting with two police superintendent in November 1979 to discuss police brutality on West Indian young people in Derby and nationally
- Letter from Derby Committee for Inter-racial solidarity requesting a meeting with DWIA. It was agreed that DWIA Secretary would make the relevant arrangements and appoint a representative to their committee.
- Commission for Racial Equality (CRE) letter inviting members to the Derby Trades Union Council May Day social event
- Jamaica Tourist Board letter received inviting DWIA members to a reception and film show in Birmingham on Tuesday 1st May 7.30pm. The Chairman and other members agreed to attend.

- Letter from Leicester United Caribbean Association seeking support for their Vincentian Appeal Fund. Committee agrees to make a cash donation
- The National Federation of Self-Help organisations invite two DWIA representatives to attend their national 2 day conference.
- Jamaica overseas UK Travel Club letter invites DWIA members to join their club

Flood Disaster in Jamaica

DWIA's Chairman and Secretary reported on the floods, and an action group in Birmingham had already begun collecting clothing for those affected. There was a challenge for the Midlands to raise £50,000, with Derby's own target being £3,000. Members recognised the difficulty of this task, but all committed to doing their best to reach the goal. It was decided that a fundraising dance would take place on Saturday 9th July at The Pennine Hotel.

The St Vincent Earthquake fund

- Members agreed to donate £10 - Leicester Caribbean Association acknowledged DWIA donation of £10 to the St Vincent Appeal Fund.
- Trinidad & Tobago republic day society letter invites DWIA members to their independence festival on Saturday 22nd September 1979
- The Chairman suggested a letter should be sent to Radio Derby, the four (4) Black roots programme Presenters, and support team thanking them for their support to promote DWIA summer Festival 1979
- The secretary reported to DWIA members on the two-day conference on funding for ethnic minority groups (London)

1985-1992

DWICA continues to provide advice and guidance sessions for members and the community on welfare, social, educational and employment matters, as well as assistance in form filling, and represent the community-on-community issues by having representation of various external bodies

Caribbean Focus 1986

This was a commonwealth Institute National body initiative and designed to celebrate the Caribbean Islands through educational activities DWIA was a member of the national committee chaired by the Mrs Ivo de Souza (former Jamaica High commission).

Regional Caribbean focus committees were then established to plan a year long programme which Derby contribution to the year-long activities included, Caribbean Island Exhibition (This exhibition complemented the Caribbean Express train that came to Derby as part of the Caribbean Focus 1986 commonwealth institute national initiative), fun run, (National flood appeal orchestrated by Jamaica High Commission – £50 raised) Gospel concert, Elders Luncheon Day, (designed to capture this old time Caribbean traditions and experience whilst having a hot Caribbean meal. Volunteers captured audio interviews / testimony of the post-world war 2 first generation of the Caribbean community in Derby.

Derby Black Business Agency

Over a period of time, DWIA held a number of meetings to establish a Derby Black Business Agency. The research study was commissioned by Black Business and completed by Ryegate Management Consultants (Sheffield). This was published in October 1988. A special mention and gratitude is due to Mr Gabbidon, who dedicated countless voluntary hours to the project.

In the wake of the 1988 Jamaican Hurricane Gilbert disaster, DWICA's Hurricane Appeal Committee (management and staff) raised an impressive £2500, which was used to buy 40 beds and mattresses, 64 boxes of good quality clothes, 3 barrels of tin food and tools. Special thanks should also be extended to Mr Cleveland Chin and Mr Walters, Mr Mighty and Mr McBean - all of whom spent a great deal of time volunteering towards the cause. DWICA staff coordinated the project and organised the logistics. £2000 was paid to the Jamaica High Commission Disaster Fund and £520 was sent directly to a school in Beacher's Town, St Ann's. The remaining funds were used to pay for shipping.

Represented by DWICA's Chairman – Mr. G. Mighty – DWICA was one of only two organisations from Britain (the other being Birmingham City Council) selected to attend a conference on immigrants and poverty in Europe at the Centre for Work & Society in Maastricht, Netherlands in November/ December 1989. This conference bore great significance for the year 1992 and the Single European Act.

- DWICA Darts team – won the Derby League Championship consecutive seasons (86-87, 87-88, & 88-89).
- DWICA made a number of successful applications to the home office regarding citizenship for African Caribbean people living in Derby.
- Telethon fundraising project – DWICA raised £80 and a special thanks to Tony Sewell Tae Kwando Group for their support

Strategic networking

Derby West Indian Association records show that from the early 1990s more strategic networking took place to respond to community issues and engage with third sector or public bodies to examine, monitor and evaluate public sector services, and to provide critical information for key stakeholders to aid decision-making. The organisations are listed below:

1992-1999

BBC East Midlands Regional Advisory Council

Commission for Racial Equality (CRE)

City Challenge

Community Health Council / Steering & Advisory Group

Community liaison with African Caribbean young people and Derby police

Community Matters (National Executive Council)

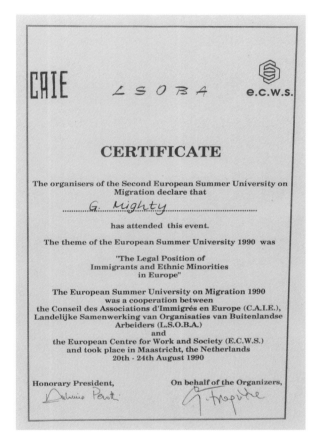

DWICA was one of two organisations (the other from Birmingham) to represent the UK at the weekend study event in Maastricht, Netherlands, in August 1990. The theme was 'The legal position of ethnic minorities in Europe' which took into consideration economic and social poverty. The event was one of many, and was part of a long process of the Maastricht Treaty which was later signed on 7 February 1992 by representatives from 12 European countries including the United Kingdom. The Treaty heralded the establishment of the European Union.

Derby University

Derbyshire County Council Minority Forum

Derby City Council Ethnic Minority Consultation Panel

Derby Black Business Project

Derby Council for Voluntary Services (CVS)

Derbyshire Ethnic Minority Forum and Community Education Support Group

Derbyshire Social Services Minority Consultation Panel

Derby City Council Education Consultation Group

Derby East Midlands Carnival Arts Partnership

Derby Minority Forum

EMCAP

Inner Area Project (IAP

Luncheon club) operates from DWICA providing support the needs of elderly African Caribbean people which is now seeing a rise in demand from the community

Multi Agency Racial Harassment Panel

National Council of Jamaicans & Supportive Organisations in UK

Pub watch / Drink wise

Southern Derbyshire Health Authority Ethnic Minority Consultative and Advisory Committee

Various housing Associations (Wall Brook & Loughborough Housing Association)

2000-2016

BBC East Midlands Regional Advisory Council

CVS

Council of Ethnic Minority Voluntary Sector Organisations

Community Matters NEC (formally NCVO)

Community Foundation Funding Panel

Community Liaison with African Caribbean young people and Derby Police

Derbyshire Multi-Agency Racial Harassment Liaison Group

Derby City Compact

Derby Racial Equality Council

Derby Community Diversity Group

Derby-Burton Cancer Network Partnership Forum

Derby Caribbean Carer's Association

Derby Black Parents Forum

Derby City Council Education – the School Organisation Committee

Derby Community Legal Service Partnership

Derbyshire Constabulary Hate Incident Review Panel

Derby City Council Minority Ethnic Communities Advisory Committee

Derby City Council Education Consultation Group

Derbyshire Ethnic Minority Forum and Community Education Support Group

Derby City Council Early Years Development Group

Derby & Derbyshire multi-Agency Racial Harassment Panel

EMCAP (East Midlands Carnival Arts partnership)

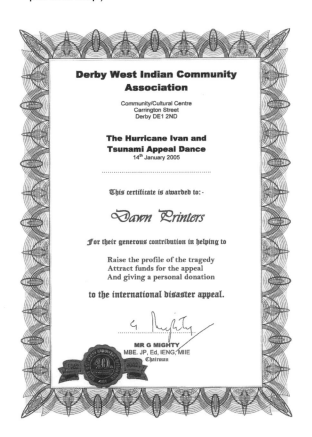

EMCCAN (East Midlands Caribbean Carnival Arts Network)

Friendship Care Housing

Hardwick Primary School

Independent Community Inclusion Board (ICIB) of Derbyshire Fire & Rescue

Immigration Advisory Service

The Jamaican Diaspora (UK)

Minority Communities Diversity Forum

Millennium volunteers

National Council of Jamaicans & Supportive Organisations in UK

Pub watch

South Derbyshire Health Authority Consultation and Advisory Committee

University of Derby

2016-2021

EMCCAN

Jamaican Diaspora UK

ICIB

University of Derby

The coronavirus pandemic

During the coronavirus pandemic, DWICA utilised digital communication technologies such as Zoom, Microsoft Teams, WhatsApp and email, as well as traditional phone calls, to host and attend meetings. They also created new services to meet the needs of the Windrush Generation and those most vulnerable during this time, such as the DWICA Covid Kitchen which provided meals, food parcels and assistance collecting medication from pharmacies. They also regularly updated their website with new information so readers could get an in-depth understanding of the organisation's services, strategic developments and activities.

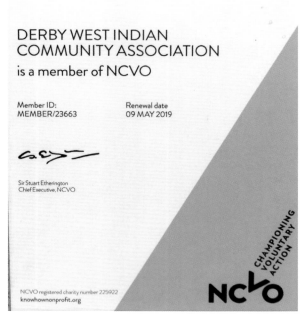

Awards and Honours

MILTON CROSDALE was awarded the OBE in October 2001 for work undertaken as a race relation officer covering the five counties of Nottinghamshire, Derbyshire, Leicestershire, Northamptonshire and Lincolnshire. He was presented with the OBE by Her Majesty, Queen Elizabeth II. He is pictured with his son and daughter.

GEORGE MIGHTY was awarded the MBE for Services to the Derby community and contributions to good Community and Race Relations in Derby in the Queen's Birthday Honours List on 15th June 1990. He was presented with the Award by Queen Elizabeth II at Buckingham Palace in November 1990.

NEZRINE HUDSON, who was Treasurer of DWICA, was awarded the MBE in the New Year's Honours List in December 1998, for Services to the West Indian Community in Derby. In March 1999, she was presented with the MBE by Queen Elizabeth II at Buckingham Palace.

ANGELLA MIGHTY was awarded the MBE in the New Year Honours List 2011 for Voluntary Service to the Derby West Indian Community Association. On 10th March 2011, she attended an Investiture at Buckingham Palace, where her award was presented to her by Queen Elizabeth II. The presentation also fell on Angella's birthday, which made the day even more special.

LLOYD NEWBY was awarded the MBE in 2014 for Voluntary Services to the Derby Communities and Contributions to Good Community Cohesion as an active member on various partnerships and bodies such as Chair of Governors (Hardwick School, Derby) and the Police Community Liaison Group.

Members of Derby's African Caribbean community who became Magistrates (Justices of the Peace)

Mr Charles Hill 1969
Mr Caleb C. McBean 1982
Mrs Edna Williamson 1983
Mr George Mighty 1990
Mrs Maureen Mosley 2005
Mrs Sharon Sewell (Scott) 2007

DWICA Chairman, George Mighty receiving the Saanjha Virsa (Shared Heritage) 'Your Community is proud of You Award' from India's Consul General, N.P. Sharma, in 2003

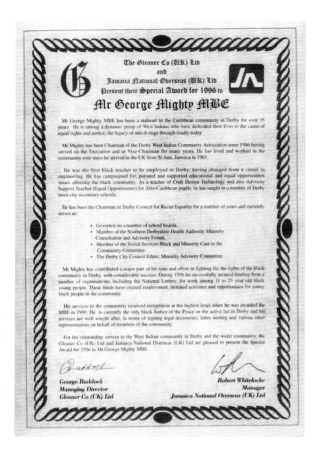

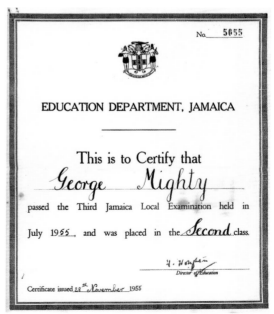

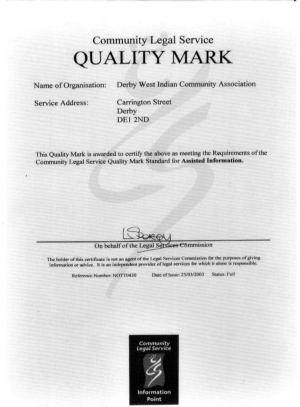

The 'Spotlight' articles are a regular feature in the annual Derby Caribbean Carnival Brochure. It is an opportunity for DWICA to publicly acknowledge the volunteers and supporters of the association.

SPOTLIGHT on

MR. G. MIGHTY

WHEN DID YOU COME TO ENGLAND?
12th September 1961 - British Overseas Airways Corporation (BOAC), arriving at London Heathrow then caught a train to Derby.

WHO INSPIRED YOU?
- Michael Mighty (my father) he inspired me in my formative years and I can remember a quote from him *"A man without education is like a man walking in the dark"*. This has been the building block which I have used throughout my working and voluntary career.
- Marcus Garvey (coming from the same parish as myself "St. Anne's" Jamaica) – his vision for the development of the African Caribbean people worldwide and being recognised as Jamaica's first national hero.
- Paulo Freire - Educator, author a Brazilian educator and philosopher who was a leading advocate of critical pedagogy (The method and practice of teaching, especially as an academic subject). He is best known for his influential work, 'Pedagogy of the Oppressed'.

EMPLOYMENT IN UK
- East Midlands Gas Board - Maintenance Engineering
- Government Training Centre - Skills Training
- Melbourne Engineering Company Limited - Production Engineering

- Derbyshire County Council - CDT Teacher
- Afro Caribbean Teacher's Association - Education Officer
- Derbyshire County Council - Advisory Teacher

WHAT WAS YOUR FIRST CAR?
In 1965 my first car was a Vauxhall Viva, then a Hillman minx, Ford Capri, Datsun 1100, Volvo 360 and now I drive a Rover 75.

WHEN DID YOU GET INVOLVED IN THE COMMUNITY SECTOR?
I was always interested in politics in Jamaica so when I came to Derby that interest continued and I educated myself on politics in Derby. In mid 1962 Mr Barnes (a pioneer founder member of DWICA) invited me to a meeting and from that day on I have been involved in improving conditions for the community, especially the African Caribbean.

WHAT HAS DWICA DONE FOR YOU?
- Made me more aware of community and diversity issues.
- It has given me a high profile based on the work I do for the community.
- What DWICA has done for everyone in the community has been to raise the profile of the community and been a conduit for community cohesion development / progression.

WHAT HAVE YOU DONE FOR DWICA?
- I have been active in DWICA over 50 years and in 1986 I was elected as DWICA Chairman. This position comes with a lot of responsibilities, fighting battles for the organisation institutionally and at a local level.
- The table highlights the representation made at strategic level to improve community cohesion.

COMMITTEES:	26
CHAIR PERSON:	6
VICE CHAIR:	2
CONSULTANT:	2
FOUNDER MEMBER:	1

- Restored DWICA as a credible organisation locally, regionally, and nationally through active participation in voluntary, public, and private sectors.

ACHIEVEMENTS/ACCOMPLISHMENTS
With a long history of community involvement spanning over 60 years we can only summarise his contribution by focusing on the key involvements:
- Secretary of Hardwick School and Community Steel Band (1977 - 1997).
- The longest serving Chairman of DWICA from 1986 to present.
- Awarded the MBE for services to the community in 1990.
- The Gleaner Company (UK) Limited and Jamaica National Building Society Overseas (UK) Limited – Special Honour Award in 1996 for his work in significantly improving the lives of the West Indian community in Derby.
- Served as a Justice of the Peace (JP) from 1991 to 2007.
- Derby City Council Civic Award 2004/5 for contribution to Racial Harmony.
- Local Heroes Award by the Institute of Jamaican Nationals Birmingham in 2007.
- Awarded the Honorary Master of the University of Derby, in January 2012 for his prodigious and remarkable record of service and achievement for the Caribbean Community and his promotion of racial harmony.

QUICK HITS (FAVOURITES)
- Dish: *Rice & Peas with Chicken or Pork*
- Fruit: *Orange*
- Vegetable: *Plantain*
- Colour: *Black*
- Sport: *Cricket*
- Drink: *Whisky & water (very seldom)*

MESSAGE FOR THE NEXT AFRICAN CARIBBEAN GENERATION
- Must have / maintain the values that have been with us for generations such as respect yourself, peers and elders. Family values are another as it gives a sense of purpose and responsibility to others.
- Be determined in order to realise your goals / success in life, whilst being resilient to overcome any barriers.
- Recognise where African Caribbean people are in the world - be aware of the history, heritage, and contribute to the legacy of development for the generation after you. Work hard / contribute to improve our condition locally, regionally, nationally and internationally.

SPOTLIGHT

This year to mark DWICA's 60th year and Derby Caribbean Carnival's 40th year milestones the spotlight shines on two people: Nezrine Hudson (below) and Egerton Perry (page 10), both longstanding members of DWICA and Volunteers of Derby Caribbean Carnival.

Nezrine was born in Mendez, St Catherine Jamaica; she came to the UK in 1966 to join her parents in Derby. Nezrine lived in the Normanton area for years before moving to Mackworth, where she now resides.

Nezrine attended Hardwick Secondary Modern Girls' School, Wilmorton College, Derbyshire College of Higher Education and Leicester Polytechnic (now university) where she studied Land Administration/Estate Management. Nezrine later attended the University Derby to study Community Development and Regeneration.

Over the years Nezrine has worked in a number of different professions, including as a Book-keeper/Secretary – Derby Diocesan Council of Education, Night Support Officer in a Women's Refuge, Community Centre Manager and Community Development Officer.

Other jobs include: Electoral Registration Officer, Census Enumerator – 1991 & 2001, Activities Co-ordinator, Part-time Youth Worker, Community Centre manager, Community Development Officer and Lunchtime Play Worker.

Nezrine has undertaken numerous voluntary work in various positions and these are just a few; Member of the National Executive Committee (NFCO), DWICA – former Trustee and Treasurer, Treasurer to a number of voluntary groups, Mentor with the Probation Service, Community Champion – Sight Support Derbyshire,

Volunteer with the Derby City Mission Night Shelter (from December to March) 2013/2014 and 2014/2015.

Nezrine's achievements include: becoming a Lieutenant in the 3rd Derby Girls' Brigade Company in the 1970's. The key milestone of this achievement was that she was the first West Indian to hold this position in Derby; President of the Derby Racial Equality Council for 2 years in the 1990's and being awarded an MBE by the Queen, for Voluntary Services to the Derby Community in 1998.

Nezrine's closing comment to inspire the next generation is that

"you can be who you want to be, providing you work hard and study hard and treat others as you would like to be treated"

EMCCAN

East Midlands Caribbean Carnival Arts Network

Donna Fox
Strategic Manager - emccan

The emccan Queen Show was hosted and produced by Derby Caribbean Carnival this year, marking their 40th Anniversary of carnival. It successfully took place at Derby Theatre on Saturday 13th June 2015. A huge thank you to all the planning group and volunteers, audience, Derby Theatre and University of Derby not to mention the contestants and designers who created magnificent costumes for this year's carnival parade!

Emccan C.I.C. is a partnership between Derby, Nottingham, Northampton and Leicester Caribbean Carnival. The organisation is based at Derby West Indian Community Centre and was formally constituted in 2012, following many years of working together. It is now in its' second phase of National Portfolio Status with regular funding from Arts Council England to support the delivery of four carnivals, a regional Queen Show and an annual publication. Emccan has confirmed continued Arts Council funding for 2015-2018, giving more security to each carnival and allowing planning time for exciting new ventures such as steel pan development, volunteer support and much more.

We are very proud to be the leading body in Caribbean Carnival arts in the East Midlands and continue to join forces with local partners and national organisations such as UKCCA, Global Carnival Centre, Greater Northern Carnival Arts Network and Carnival Network South, and advocate for the very best quality in carnival arts delivery!!!

Incredible progress has been made both artistically and organisationally over the past three years. This has set firm foundations for us to plan more carnival related activities throughout the year, such as a regional carnival conference and youth music programme, developing carnival arts year round and not just in carnival season.

Emccan has worked with local artists and troupes over winter months to help raise over £94,000, so far, through fundraising surgeries in association with Arts Council England and UKCCA. This will enhance the parades, with many troupes touring the UK throughout 2015. It is an honour working with such dedicated and passionate people to extend artistic boundaries and raise the level of artistic quality in East Midlands carnival parades.

SPOTLIGHT

on Milton Fitzroy Crosdale

When did you come to England?

In the Winter months just after Jamaica got its independence in 1962.

My Parent were already in the UK Nottingham since 1954 so I arrived at our family home on a cold winter's night. The cost of the air fare was £75, and I was 19 years old.

Quick hits what is your favourites:

Dish:	Jamaican National Dish - Ackee & Salt-fish Regular/nowadays Fish/rice/pasta/curries
Drink:	Red wine / Guinness and now Tonic Water
Colour:	Green
Sport:	Cricket
First Car:	Ford Cortina Mk. 1

Who inspired you?

- My Grandfather who was a Lay Pastor and a well travelled person visiting Cuba, Panama and many other Caribbean countries. Came back to Jamaica to resume farming.
- Sir Alexander Bustamante Trade union leader and former prime minister of Jamaica (the first prime minister of Jamaica 1962).He founded the Bustamante Industrial Trade Union following the 1938 labour riots, and the Jamaican Labour Party in 1943. Bustamante is honoured in Jamaica with the title National Hero of Jamaica in recognition of his achievements.
- Norman Washington Manley was a barrister and leader of the PNP (People's National Party) and also a former prime minister of Jamaica.

- Eric Irons – A fellow Jamaican... the first Black JP in Nottingham and the UK after the 1958 race riots.
- Lord David Pitt, Baron Pitt of Hampstead, He was a general practitioner, a labour peer remained an activist championing the cause of equal rights throughout his life.

Key Accomplishments

- Working for the Race Relations Board around 1969 after the 1965 Race Relation Act.
- Working as Race Relations Officer covering five counties including, in the main Derbyshire, Nottinghamshire, Leicestershire, Northamptonshire, and Lincolnshire.
- Working with different communities to secure the development of a community facility e.g. DWICA phase 2 (main hall section). For the Indian and Pakistani communities, the development of their respective community centres.
- Arrange visit for Sir George Young to Derby (who was responsible for the Urban Programme)
- In Nottingham assisted in the fundraising and development of The Afro-Caribbean National Artistic (ACNA) centre and the Indian & Pakistani community centres.
- Visit by Prince Charles to Derby on Friday 27th February 1981. This entailed working in partnership with Buckingham Palace staff, Derby Lord Lieutenant (the Queen's local representative) to plan the itinerary for the day that included visiting Madeley Centre.
- In 1980/81 – Worked in partnership to fund raise with the Indian Community Centre to purchase a Dialysis machine for Derby Royal Infirmary (DRI)
- 1985 – Nottingham Senior Community Relations Officer to address racial matters/incidents that warranted investigation.
- Elected to Derbyshire County Council and to Derby City Council and became vice chairman to the Social Services Committee

- 1983 Village School – Board of governors - vice chair, sat on Board of governors Hardwick School
- Member of Derbyshire Police Authority
- Policy Development with key employers in Derby Rolls Royce, British Celanese, British Rail, Toyota to ensure racial matters were dealt with correctly and social matters such as ensuring Minority ethnic people had access to employment and progression in work.
- 2001 – Receiving an OBE from the Queen.

Milton on day of receiving his OBE alongside his son and daughter

Working in Nottingham

- Campaigning in Nottingham to ensure that various communities had better access to education and to reduce the rate of school expulsion
- Working with communities to increase the number of Asian and Caribbean people serving on the school governing bodies
- Served on a number of public bodies including Local Skills Council (LSC).
- Became the first African Caribbean governor at Clarendon College 1986/87
- Chaired Afro Caribbean National Artistic Centre (ACNA) centre for 12 years
- Chaired the Nottingham West Indian Student Union, and later became chair of the Commonwealth Citizen Association (later known as the West Indian National Association)
- Currently chairing PATRA (Positive Action Training for young black people)

What has DWICA done for you?

Being part of one of the oldest black organization in Derby. It gave me a sense of satisfaction that the organisation was able to help the community to achieve their aspiration whether in education, business, social recreation (cricket and dominoes)

The organisation helped cared for the community by purchasing a burial plot (Nottingham Road cemetery) to ensure that community members who had come up against hard times were not given a pauper's funeral. DWICA continues to provide a forum for social action and cultural experiences like carnival.

Message for the next generation:

Quote from my Grandmother
"Aim for the sky and you will reach the clouds"
(have ambition)

- If going into business you should have a clear sense of the goals that you wish to achieve and seek the necessary assistance you require.
- Do not forget your educational goals
- Have a good educational based to ensure a long-term career
- Parents should always create a road map for their children and grandchildren.
- Ensure have a clear sense of cohesion within the community so that we support and encourage each other that we celebrate people's life while they are alive
- We should ensure that we create a viable environment to care for our growing elderly community.
- We should write our own history, don't let other people write it for us

Closing Remarks

We as a community need to encourage and support our young people to be engaged in local and national politics to represent the BME community. Black led churches and other dominations are best placed to encourage this type action.

[Left to right] Mr. Eric Irons, George Powe, Micheal Manley (JA former Prime Minister), Tony Robinson, Milton Crosdale

4 01332 371529 INFO@DWICA.CO.UK WWW.DWICA.CO.UK 5

SPOTLIGHT CONT'D

Egerton Perry was born in St. Catherine Jamaica and came to England in 1967. He has resided in Derby since that time.

His biggest culture shock on coming to England was the snow, as coming from the Caribbean there was no snow, so seeing it and experiencing the cold was a big culture shock to him.

Egerton attended Pear Tree Boys' School for two years.

His favourite dish is pea soup and favourite hard food roast yam. Egerton loves Lord Nelson mangoes as they are big and sweet and his favourite tipple is Jameson whisky.

Egerton's role model and mentor is Michael Holding and he had the opportunity to take him on local visits

when Michael was playing cricket for Derbyshire. He was impressed with Michael as he was a conscious man who adopted a calm, collected and positive approach to life.

His first job was as an Apprentice Joiner at Edward Woods & Son, Park Street. He also worked at Leeds Foundry - Fork Lift Driver (it was at this job where he learnt to drive a car), Rolls Royce – Machine Operator and as a Self -employed Taxi Driver.

In 1998 Egerton became involved with DWICA when he was employed as a full-time caretaker. He was with DWICA for 16 years.

Egerton has also undertaken a number of voluntary roles, such as maintaining the

Domino team at DWICA for over 10 years and being a member of the Derby Caribbean Carnival Planning group, helping to organise and plan the two day event.

Egerton's closing comments to inspire the next generation is to **"Study hard and have a good education, have good self-appearance (clean and tidy) and to respect each other"**

THE PROCESSION

THIS YEAR'S THEME
FAMILY & COMMUNITY

PROGRAMME

Procession - Day 1
Saturday 18th July 2015
1.00 pm Procession starts from Pear Tree Junior School
3.00 pm Procession reaches the Market Place
3.10 pm Costume Competition/Exhibition
5.00 pm Stage Show - Local Talents
6.00 pm End

Carnival - Day 2
Sunday 19th July 2015
1.00 pm Official Opening
1.10 pm Stage Show begins

Route
1. Pear Tree Street
2. Portland Street
3. St. Thomas Road
4. Pear Tree Road
5. Normanton Road
6. Babington Lane
7. St. Peter's Street
8. The Market Place

10 01332 371529 INFO@DWICA.CO.UK WWW.DWICA.CO.UK 11

TRIBUTE TO MR. CALEB McBEAN

The Derby West Indian Community Association, Management and Membership mourn the passing of Mr. Caleb McBean who died in Jamaica on 8 March 2014.

We are pleased and happy to say one of our members, Mr. Willitz Gabbidon, who was in Jamaica at the time, was able to attend the funeral and present flowers on the Association's behalf.

Mr. McBean was one of the founder members of the Derby West Indian Community Association. Although the first seed of the organisation was sown in 1955, the Association proper was formed in December 1961 and Mr. McBean was elected as its first Treasurer.

Mr. McBean served the Association in the capacity as Treasurer, Secretary and Vice Chairman, before retiring to Jamaica in 1996 after 40 years in England.

His great energy and enthusiasm for voluntary community work and fighting inequality was unfaltering. He served on a variety of committees in the City of Derby and represented the Association at various civic and social functions/events. His objective to provide a community and public service and his desire for social justice is evidenced by his work in the church and his service as one of the first Black Magistrates to serve on the Southern Derbyshire Magistrate Bench.

In terms of the development of the Association's work and status he has made significant contributions through all stages, from its formation to the establishment of the community cultural centre.

It is interesting to note that the footage to the film "The Carnival" in 2010 was provided by Mr. McBean who had kept these reel films he made at carnival in the 1970's. His legacy is, therefore, one from which our community will continue to benefit for generations to come.

It was a pleasure to work with him over those many years.

G Mighty
Chairman of the Committee of Managing Trustees
Derby West Indian Community Association

SAMANTHA IN BRAZIL

Funded by the Arts Council England, Samantha Hudson was invited to work behind the scenes of Brazil Carnival 2014 by Gandaia Arts and travelled along the East coast of Brazil researching Carnival history while taking part in a variety of workshops from Maracatu Dance, Drumming, Puppet Making, Samba dancing and Carnival & disabilities.

For a Photographic documentary visit the 'from Derby to Brazil Carnival 2014' website: **samcarnival.wordpress.com**.

In Rio, Samantha attended lectures at the University of Rio de Janeiro on float design & making, the structures of the Carnival procession past and present, Costumes design & make for Queens and troupes, and addressing the scoring system for competitions.

Whilst in Pernambuco, Brazil, Samantha visited orphanage and spent time with Founder / Director, Cleonice Silvia who began with 1 room, 1 kilo of rice, 1 kilo of black beans and 70 children. 20 years on Cleonice has 80 children and 5 volunteer staff in her home.

In support for the children there was a "Skate & Donate" community fundraising event on Saturday 7th June and all proceeds will go to the children of Crèche Tancredo Neves orphanage in Pernambuco, Brazil. Event dress code, Brazil flag colours: YELLOW, BLUE, GREEN & WHITE for support.

For more information on how you can support contact Sam Carnival **s.l.s.hudson1@gmail.com**

Professor Cecile Wright is the newly appointed member of the Jamaican Diaspora Advisory Board representing the UK (North) for the period of 2014-2016. The constituency covers citizens of Jamaican background in Birmingham, Wolverhampton, Nottingham, Derby, Leicester, Burton, Sheffield, Leeds, Huddersfield, Northampton and Luton. The function of the Board is to advise the Jamaican Minister of State with responsibility for Jamaican Oversees Community, on issues relating to the Diaspora. As a member of the Board, I work with community groups in order to acquire an understanding of issues/ interests and concerns, liaise with the Jamaican High Commissioner, assists with the planning of all Diaspora Conferences and attend Board meeting in Jamaica to report on and discuss matters of relevant to the Diaspora.

The Jamaican Diaspora UK is hosting a conference themed 'Our Heritage, Our Legacy'. 13-15 June 2014, to be held in Birmingham. Its focus will include issues relating to, 'Youth Education and Employment, Health, Crime and Security in Jamaica'.

I look forward to seeing you at the conference for what promises to be a good event.

If you wish to invite me to future events in your area, have any queries or wish to discuss pertinent matters, please send an email to: **cecile.wright@jamaicandiasporauk.org**.

CECILE WRIGHT

SPOTLIGHT ON

STAX MOTOR SERVICES

Derby Caribbean carnival in its support of local businesses this year has put the spotlight on one of the longest serving African Caribbean Businesses in Derby, Stax Motor Services, and as such interviewed the owner & proprietor **Mr Lloyd Newby**

Name of Business: STAX MOTOR SERVICES
Location: Upperdale Road (Cavendish Island) Derby, Derbyshire, DE23 8BQ

Business: Car servicing and repairs
Telephone Number: 01332 771185
Opening Hours:
Monday – Friday 8.30am – 5.30pm
Saturday 8.30am – 1.00pm

When was Stax Motor Services formed?
In October 1979
1st location - Arch Unit 8 Friar Gate Bridge (1979)
2nd location – Robinson Industrial Estate, Shaftesbury Street (1981)
3rd location – Cavendish Island 1982

Why was Stax Motor Services formed?
As a worker of Mann Egerton Littleover at the time (1979) I was covering for the foreman and got to see the work cards for the cars the mechanics had worked on and the cost they (Mann Egerton) charged to their customers. Based on this it was clear that in one day mechanics would make their wages for the week and the other four days' worked would be for the company. It was clear then that I wanted to work for myself and not for a company.

Why the name Stax Motor Services?
At the time Stax records was a record label known for creating Southern and Memphis soul music styles along with Gospel funk and Jazz recordings which was a label that promoted African American music. It was commonly listened to during the 1960's & 70's. This was the basis of calling the company Stax Motor Services.

What was life like for a mechanic in those days?
All mechanics had to have their own tools which enabled them to do and complete work on cars of the day. Mobile tool companies would visit motor mechanics place of work and sell tools to them on credit with an agreed weekly payment plan. By having the tools it was possible to meet the time allocation to the work to be undertaken as detailed in motor service manuals such as EMI manual that gave the times for car service and repair jobs. If you were a good mechanic you could complete the job within the allocated time and accredit that time to the next job and in doing so could develop a time bank which would allow for additional work to be undertaken hence receiving a bonus payment for such additional work.

What Cars did Stax Motor Services specialise in, in the early days?
• Triumph 2.5 injection
• Triumph TR 5 & 6
• Rover 3500 s
• Jaguar XJ6
• Lucas fuel injection systems

What has kept Stax Motor Services going for so long?
This is a question that I have been asked a number of times and there is no simple answer to this but I will give you a summary:-
The **location** at Cavendish Island has been a key factor. When the petrol station was operating there was a lot of passing trade by customers who bought petrol and they would book their cars in for servicing or have repair work done.
Providing a **good service to customers at an affordable rate** has and continues to be important and this promotes the business to new customers and for repeat business. Offering motor advice for those enthusiasts who are avid DIY people also created a positive business image that enabled Stax Motor Services to be known within the community.
Stax Motor Services is a point of reference for networking with other businesses within the community and as such has signposted customers to companies or agencies that can help them (with non-motor mechanical needs).
At times Stax Motor Services have been informal mentors for customers in need of moral support and guidance when faced with life challenges. To do so Staff have developed listening skills which comes from listening to BBC Radio 4 for over 30 years in which presenters discuss topic of current affairs and provide advice or solutions on matters of radio interest.
Responding to business opportunities is also a key factor "being at the right place at the right time" such as moving location as was the case for Stax Motor Services moving from Robinson Industrial Estate (Shaftesbury street) to Cavendish Island.

Developing Stax Motor Services – what has this process taught you?
As a person that owns his own company there are sacrifices that has to be made in the early years to establish the business and to keep it running. In my case I had to learn quickly "on the Job" about:-
• Self-employment
• VAT & businesses
• HMRC & businesses
• Legality (relevant to businesses)
• Local authority planning permission procedure
• Financial management
• Business banking
• Business insurance
• Leasing & Purchasing property
• Purchasing equipment
• Business planning (including (marketing & promotion)
• Corporate social responsibility (CSR)
• Increasing business knowledge and understanding, by reading local and national papers / journals. Attending seminars/ events relevant to the motor trade
• Work placement Tutor – through a partnership with Wilmorton College (as it was known then) Stax Motor Services delivered a twelve (12) weeks work placements for two (2) young people (at any one time) to gain valuable work experience as a motor mechanic. This continued for a five (5) year period

Future of Stax Motor Services
Continue trading and serve the people of Derby to meet their motoring needs.

Voluntary work/ Achievements
Chair of Governors (Hardwick Primary School Normanton)

IAG critical friend looking at the police service in Derbyshire

Police Authority, serving on the board since 2006 and during this time sat on the interview panel for Police Chief Constable, Assistant Chief Constable and Support Chief Constable.

Stax Motor Services - It has been a journey in which I am proud of as I can recall where I have come from to where I am now

Employees and Volunteers, Past and Present

Anita Lewis – Youth Worker
Leo Bennett – Manager
Jenny Duncan – caretaker
Peter Durham – Caretaker
Kenneth Wray – Caretaker
Lance – Caretaker
Egerton Perry – Caretaker
Lloyd Douce – Bar Manager
Windell Hinds – Bar Manager
Vincent Sewell – Bar Manager
Vin Goulburne – Bar Manager
Janet Goulburne – Bar Assistant

Kevin Brown – Assistant Manager
Madline McDonald – Project Admin staff
Julie Wright – Project Admin staff
Linton Douce – Project Worker
Paulet Harris – Project Assistant
Everton Haslam – Project Worker
Helen Myrie – Development Officer
Loxley Ford – Development Officer
Samantha Hudson – Project Assistant
(Mother & Baby Group)
Don Trubshaw - Education Officer
Annett Johnson – Education Assistant

The present DWICA Management Committee. Seated (L-R): George Mighty, Adaline Palmer, Gloria Wilks; Second row (L-R): Mable Slater, Mica Barrett, Professor Cecile Wright, Monica Dean, Angella Mighty, Maureen Mosley, Nezrine Hudson (Centre Manager); Back row (L-R): Pamela Samuel, Lloyd Newby.

Trevor Brown – Centre Manager
Takyiwa Sankofa, Youth & Community
Outreach Worker
Berimma Sankofa – Project Manager
Nezrine Hudson – Project Manager
Janet Niangoma – Volunteer Admin
Michael Codrington – Centre Manager
Margaret Brown – Youth Worker
Lydia Grigdion – Centre Manager
Kate Lee – Assistant Manager
Adam Slater – Project Officer (Elders)
Danielle Vassell, Project Officer (Elders)
Jordan Rhule-Campbell – Project Officer
(CYP)
Hollie White – Project Officer (CYP)
Charis Beoku-Betts – Project Manager
William Farrell – Administrator

SUMMER SCHOOL STAFF

Errol Cover – Co-ordinator
Madge Spencer
Delroy Taylor
Rachel Box
Belvir Sandhu
Amanda Percy
David Marr
Michelle Henry-Morgan
Siobhan Coleman
Michael Campbell
Nana Panti-Amoa
Leonie Panti-Amoa
Ogochukwu Ejiofor (Ogo)
Nadine Mighty
Carol Cooper
Niaz Stephenson
Tamara Rashford
Alex Johnson
Stacey Mighty
Julie Spence
Alison Solomon
Amoy Johnson
Ellen Feron – Summer School Volunteer

VOLUNTEERS

Virinder 'Bimmy' Rai – In 2013 conducted a research / survey analysis, and produced a report into *"The Health Needs of the African and Caribbean Community in Derby"* for DWICA. This resulted in the establishment of DWICA's 'Active Health Lives Matter' project attracting funding from Derby City Public Health and Lottery Health Trust consistently for six years. She also helps DWICA secure additional Resources for the Organisation.
Jackie Williams – Carnival Volunteer Admin
Rachael Francois – Carnival Volunteer Admin